Hands-On Python wit

A Practical Guide for Beginners

Sarful Hasssan

Preface

Welcome to **"Hands-On Python with Fastai: A Practical Guide for Beginners"**! This book offers a practical, step-by-step approach to learning machine learning using Python and Fastai, making it perfect for beginners. You'll start with Python fundamentals, explore the Fastai library, and complete hands-on projects such as **image classification** and **sentiment analysis**.

Who This Book Is For

This book is for anyone interested in learning **machine learning** and **deep learning** with Python and Fastai, especially beginners with little or no experience in AI. It's also great for those who want to implement cutting-edge techniques like **transfer learning** and **fine-tuning**.

How This Book Is Organized

- **Part 1**: Introduction to Python and Fastai
- **Part 2**: Practical projects, including **image classification** and **text analysis**

- **Part 3**: Advanced topics and **model deployment** using **Flask** and **FastAPI**

Each chapter builds on the previous one to give you a hands-on, practical learning experience.

What Was Left Out

This book focuses on practical applications and doesn't delve deeply into advanced topics like model architectures or low-level optimizations. It's intended to help you build functional AI models quickly.

Code Style

The code follows **PEP 8** standards for clarity and maintainability, with clear explanations. Example code is available for download to help you practice.

Release Notes

The book is designed for the latest versions of **Python** and **Fastai**. Some code may need adjustments if you're using newer versions of these libraries.

MechatronicsLAB Online Learning
For additional resources and courses in **AI** and **robotics**, visit mechatronicslab.net.

How to Contact Us
Questions? Feedback? Email us at mechatronicslab@gmail.com.

Acknowledgments
Thanks to the **Fastai** and **Python** communities for their invaluable contributions, and to the **MechatronicsLAB** team for their support.

Disclaimer
While every effort has been made to ensure the accuracy of the content, the author and publisher are not responsible for any errors or omissions.

Table of Contents

Chapter - 1 Introduction to Python and Fastai

Python and Fastai form a powerful combination for deep learning enthusiasts and professionals. Fastai simplifies the development of high-performance neural networks, enabling users to focus on results rather than low-level details.

Why Python?

Python is the backbone of modern machine learning and deep learning due to:

- **Ease of Use**: Python's clean syntax makes it accessible to both beginners and experts.
- **Extensive Libraries**: Python's ecosystem includes TensorFlow, PyTorch, and Fastai, which are integral to deep learning.
- **Community Support**: A large and active community ensures a wealth of resources, tutorials, and libraries.

What is Fastai? Fastai is a high-level library built on PyTorch, designed to make deep learning accessible and effective. It abstracts the complexities of PyTorch while retaining its flexibility, enabling rapid prototyping and experimentation.

Key Features of Fastai

- **Ease of Use**: Provides high-level APIs for common tasks like image classification, text analysis, and tabular data modeling.
- **Built-in Best Practices**: Incorporates state-of-the-art techniques, such as data augmentation, transfer learning, and mixed-precision training.
- **Flexibility**: Allows seamless customization and low-level control by interacting directly with PyTorch.
- **Rich Documentation**: Includes detailed guides, tutorials, and example notebooks.

Why Use Python with Fastai?

1. **Integration with PyTorch**: Fastai is built on PyTorch, ensuring compatibility with one of the most powerful deep learning frameworks.
2. **Rapid Prototyping**: Simplifies the process of creating, training, and deploying models.

3. **Community and Support**: Extensive resources are available, including the Fastai forums and course materials.

Python and Fastai make deep learning approachable without sacrificing performance or flexibility. Whether you're a beginner exploring neural networks or an expert optimizing advanced models, this duo empowers you to achieve your goals efficiently.

Installing and Setting Up Fastai

Setting up Fastai is simple and straightforward, and it integrates seamlessly with the PyTorch ecosystem. Follow these steps to install and configure it for your deep learning projects:

Step 1: Install Python Ensure Python is installed on your system. Download the latest version from the official Python website. During installation, select the option to add Python to your system PATH.

Step 2: Install PyTorch Fastai depends on PyTorch, so it must be installed first. Visit the PyTorch website to find the appropriate installation command for your system, CUDA version, and package manager. For example:

- For CPU-only support: `pip install torch torchvision torchaudio`
- For GPU support: `pip install torch torchvision torchaudio --index-url https://download.pytorch.org/whl/cu118`

Step 3: Install Fastai Once PyTorch is installed, install Fastai using pip:
`pip install fastai`
To upgrade to the latest version, use:
`pip install --upgrade fastai`

Installing Fastai on Different Platforms

Windows:

- Ensure Python and pip are updated.
- Follow the standard PyTorch and Fastai installation commands as listed above.

Linux:

- Open a terminal and install PyTorch and Fastai using pip: `pip install torch torchvision torchaudio`
  `pip install fastai`

- For advanced use cases, consider setting up a virtual environment using venv or conda.

macOS:
- Use pip to install PyTorch and Fastai, ensuring compatibility with the macOS environment.

Anaconda:
1. Create a new environment for Fastai: `conda create -n fastai_env python=3.9`
   `conda activate fastai_env`
2. Install PyTorch using conda: `conda install pytorch torchvision torchaudio pytorch-cuda=11.8 -c pytorch -c nvidia`
3. Install Fastai: `pip install fastai`

Step 4: Verify Installation After installation, verify that Fastai is set up correctly:

```
from fastai.vision.all import *
print("Fastai successfully installed.")
```

If no errors occur, Fastai is ready for use.

Step 5: Install Supporting Libraries Fastai works best with additional libraries for data manipulation and visualization:
- **Pandas:** `pip install pandas`
- **Matplotlib** and **Seaborn:** `pip install matplotlib seaborn`

Step 6: Test Fastai Run a simple example to ensure everything is working correctly:

```
from fastai.vision.all import *

# Load a sample dataset
path = untar_data(URLs.PETS)/'images'
dls = ImageDataLoaders.from_name_re(path,
get_image_files(path), pat=r'(.+)_\d+.jpg',
item_tfms=Resize(224))

# Train a model
learn = vision_learner(dls, resnet34,
metrics=error_rate)
learn.fine_tune(1)
```

If the script runs successfully and trains a model, your Fastai setup is complete.

With Fastai installed and tested, you are ready to build and deploy advanced deep learning models effortlessly.

Overview of Fastai's Features and Philosophy

Fastai is a deep learning library that stands out for its simplicity and effectiveness. Built on top of PyTorch, Fastai offers a high-level API that abstracts the complexities of deep learning while still providing the flexibility for advanced users. Its design philosophy centers on accessibility, performance, and state-of-the-art practices.

Core Features of Fastai

1. **Ease of Use**:
    a. High-level APIs simplify common tasks like data loading, model training, and evaluation.
    b. Minimal boilerplate code allows users to quickly prototype models.
2. **Comprehensive Preprocessing Tools**:
    a. Robust data augmentation techniques for images, text, and tabular data.
    b. Built-in support for handling missing values, categorical encoding, and normalization for tabular data.
3. **Model Training**:
    a. Includes a wide range of pre-trained models for transfer learning.
    b. Implements techniques like learning rate finder, discriminative learning rates, and progressive resizing.
4. **Interoperability with PyTorch**:
    a. Seamless integration with PyTorch, allowing low-level customizations and advanced control.
    b. Users can easily switch between Fastai's high-level APIs and PyTorch's core functionalities.
5. **Extensive Metrics and Visualizations**:
    a. Built-in metrics like accuracy, precision, recall, and F1 score.

      b. Tools for visualizing learning rates, losses, and model predictions.

6. **Support for Multiple Data Types**:
      a. Handles diverse data types, including images, text, tabular data, and time-series data.
      b. Unified interface for working with these data types simplifies the workflow.

7. **Modular Design**:
      a. Enables users to use individual components independently, such as data loaders or model architectures.
      b. Encourages reusability and customization.

8. **Fastai Callback System**:
      a. Provides hooks to modify training behavior dynamically.
      b. Includes built-in callbacks for tasks like early stopping, mixed-precision training, and scheduling learning rates.

Philosophy of Fastai

1. **Democratizing Deep Learning**:
      a. Fastai aims to make deep learning accessible to everyone, regardless of their technical background.
      b. Offers free courses, documentation, and tutorials to lower the entry barrier.

2. **Performance-Oriented Design**:
      a. Prioritizes speed and efficiency without sacrificing simplicity.
      b. Leverages modern hardware like GPUs and techniques such as mixed-precision training to accelerate computations.

3. **State-of-the-Art Practices by Default**:
      a. Incorporates the latest advancements in deep learning research.
      b. Examples include differential learning rates, transfer learning, and data augmentation techniques.

4. **Flexibility and Extensibility**:
      a. Empowers users to go beyond pre-built functions and create custom workflows.

    b. Designed to work seamlessly with PyTorch for low-level experimentation.

5. **Community-Driven Development**:
    a. Actively maintained and improved by an engaged community of developers and researchers.
    b. Feedback-driven updates ensure the library evolves with user needs.

Fastai's blend of accessibility, power, and cutting-edge techniques makes it a compelling choice for deep learning practitioners. Whether you're building a simple classification model or experimenting with custom architectures, Fastai offers the tools to streamline and enhance your workflow.

Overview of Fastai's Features and Philosophy

Fastai is a deep learning library that stands out for its simplicity and effectiveness. Built on top of PyTorch, Fastai offers a high-level API that abstracts the complexities of deep learning while still providing the flexibility for advanced users. Its design philosophy centers on accessibility, performance, and state-of-the-art practices.

Core Features of Fastai

1. **Ease of Use**:
    a. High-level APIs simplify common tasks like data loading, model training, and evaluation.
    b. Minimal boilerplate code allows users to quickly prototype models.

2. **Comprehensive Preprocessing Tools**:
    a. Robust data augmentation techniques for images, text, and tabular data.
    b. Built-in support for handling missing values, categorical encoding, and normalization for tabular data.

3. **Model Training**:
    a. Includes a wide range of pre-trained models for transfer learning.
    b. Implements techniques like learning rate finder, discriminative learning rates, and progressive resizing.

4. **Interoperability with PyTorch**:
    a. Seamless integration with PyTorch, allowing low-level

customizations and advanced control.

b. Users can easily switch between Fastai's high-level APIs and PyTorch's core functionalities.

5. **Extensive Metrics and Visualizations:**

a. Built-in metrics like accuracy, precision, recall, and F1 score.

b. Tools for visualizing learning rates, losses, and model predictions.

6. **Support for Multiple Data Types:**

a. Handles diverse data types, including images, text, tabular data, and time-series data.

b. Unified interface for working with these data types simplifies the workflow.

7. **Modular Design:**

a. Enables users to use individual components independently, such as data loaders or model architectures.

b. Encourages reusability and customization.

8. **Fastai Callback System:**

a. Provides hooks to modify training behavior dynamically.

b. Includes built-in callbacks for tasks like early stopping, mixed-precision training, and scheduling learning rates.

Philosophy of Fastai

1. **Democratizing Deep Learning:**

a. Fastai aims to make deep learning accessible to everyone, regardless of their technical background.

b. Offers free courses, documentation, and tutorials to lower the entry barrier.

2. **Performance-Oriented Design:**

a. Prioritizes speed and efficiency without sacrificing simplicity.

b. Leverages modern hardware like GPUs and techniques such as mixed-precision training to accelerate computations.

3. **State-of-the-Art Practices by Default:**

a. Incorporates the latest advancements in deep learning research.

b. Examples include differential learning rates, transfer learning, and data augmentation techniques.

4. **Flexibility and Extensibility**:

   a. Empowers users to go beyond pre-built functions and create custom workflows.

   b. Designed to work seamlessly with PyTorch for low-level experimentation.

5. **Community-Driven Development**:

   a. Actively maintained and improved by an engaged community of developers and researchers.

   b. Feedback-driven updates ensure the library evolves with user needs.

Applications of Fastai

Fastai's capabilities enable its use across various domains, solving real-world problems with ease and efficiency. Below are some key applications:

1. **Computer Vision**:

   a. Image classification (e.g., identifying objects in images).

   b. Object detection for tasks like facial recognition or vehicle tracking.

   c. Image segmentation for medical imaging and autonomous driving.

2. **Natural Language Processing (NLP)**:

   a. Sentiment analysis for customer feedback or social media data.

   b. Language translation and text generation.

   c. Document classification, such as spam filtering or legal document categorization.

3. **Tabular Data Analysis**:

   a. Predictive modeling for structured datasets in finance, healthcare, and retail.

   b. Handling missing data, feature engineering, and data cleaning.

4. **Time-Series Forecasting**:

    a. Applications in stock market prediction, weather forecasting, and demand planning.

5. **Recommendation Systems**:
    a. Building systems to recommend movies, products, or services based on user behavior.

6. **Education and Research**:
    a. Simplifies experimentation with deep learning models for academic research.
    b. Provides a foundation for learning through interactive tutorials and examples.

7. **Healthcare**:
    a. Medical image analysis for disease detection and diagnosis.
    b. Predicting patient outcomes using structured and unstructured data.

8. **Autonomous Systems**:
    a. Training models for robotics and autonomous vehicles.
    b. Enhancing performance in real-time decision-making systems.

Fastai's blend of accessibility, power, and cutting-edge techniques makes it a compelling choice for deep learning practitioners. Whether you're building a simple classification model or experimenting with custom architectures, Fastai offers the tools to streamline and enhance your workflow.

Understanding Fastai's Layered API Design

Fastai's layered API design is a standout feature that caters to users of all experience levels, from beginners to advanced developers. By organizing its functionality into layers, Fastai allows users to engage with the library at the level of abstraction that suits their needs.

1. High-Level API The high-level API is designed for simplicity and ease of use. It abstracts complex deep learning tasks into a few lines of code, making it ideal for beginners or those looking for rapid prototyping. Features:

- Pre-built functions for common tasks such as data loading, model creation, and training.
- State-of-the-art practices like transfer learning and data

augmentation are applied automatically.

Example:

```
from fastai.vision.all import *
# Load dataset
path = untar_data(URLs.PETS)/'images'
dls = ImageDataLoaders.from_name_re(path,
get_image_files(path), pat=r'(.+)_\d+.jpg',
item_tfms=Resize(224))
# Create and train a model
learn = vision_learner(dls, resnet34,
metrics=error_rate)
learn.fine_tune(1)
```

2. Mid-Level API The mid-level API provides more control while retaining ease of use. It allows users to customize specific parts of the deep learning pipeline, such as data processing and training loops.

Features:

- Flexibility to modify individual components like data augmentations or optimizers.
- Access to callbacks for dynamic training adjustments.

Example:

```
from fastai.vision.augment import aug_transforms
# Custom data augmentation
item_tfms = Resize(224)
batch_tfms = aug_transforms(mult=2.0)
dls = ImageDataLoaders.from_name_re(path,
get_image_files(path), pat=r'(.+)_\d+.jpg',

item_tfms=item_tfms, batch_tfms=batch_tfms)
learn = vision_learner(dls, resnet34, metrics=accuracy)
learn.fit_one_cycle(3)
```

3. Low-Level API The low-level API offers granular control, enabling users to build custom workflows from scratch. It is suited for advanced users who need to experiment with unique data types, model architectures, or training techniques.

Features:

- Direct access to PyTorch's core functionalities.
- Fully customizable training loops, data loaders, and models.

Example:

```python
from fastai.vision.core import PILImage
from fastai.data.block import DataBlock
from fastai.learner import Learner
from fastai.optimizer import Adam
# Define a custom DataBlock
blocks = DataBlock(blocks=(ImageBlock, CategoryBlock),
                   get_items=get_image_files,
splitter=RandomSplitter(),
                   get_y=parent_label,
item_tfms=Resize(128))
# Create DataLoaders
path = untar_data(URLs.PETS)/'images'
dls = blocks.dataloaders(path)
# Define a custom learner
learn = Learner(dls, resnet34(), opt_func=Adam,
loss_func=CrossEntropyLossFlat(), metrics=accuracy)
learn.fit(5)
```

Why Layered API Design Matters

1. **Accessibility**: Beginners can start with the high-level API and achieve results without needing deep technical expertise.
2. **Flexibility**: Advanced users can drop to lower layers to implement custom workflows.
3. **Scalability**: Users can gradually learn and transition to more complex features as their expertise grows.
4. **Efficiency**: The layered structure streamlines the development process, enabling faster experimentation and deployment.

Fastai's layered API design ensures that the library is approachable yet powerful, making it a valuable tool for diverse use cases and skill levels.

Understanding DataBlock API in Fastai

The DataBlock API is one of Fastai's most powerful and flexible tools for building data pipelines. It provides a structured way to define how data should be processed and loaded, catering to a variety of data types and use cases.

Key Concepts of DataBlock API

1. **Blocks**:
    a. Specify the types of input and output for your model.
    b. Commonly used blocks include:
        i. ImageBlock: For image data.
        ii. TextBlock: For text data.
        iii. CategoryBlock: For categorical labels.
        iv. RegressionBlock: For continuous numerical targets.
2. **Getters**:
    a. Define how to retrieve the items (e.g., file paths) and labels from your dataset.
    b. Functions like get_image_files or custom methods can be used.
3. **Splitters**:
    a. Determine how the dataset is split into training and validation sets.
    b. Examples include RandomSplitter, GrandparentSplitter, or custom splitting logic.
4. **Item and Batch Transforms**:
    a. Apply transformations to individual items or batches of data.
    b. Examples include resizing, cropping, and normalization.

Defining a DataBlock A DataBlock is defined by combining these components into a reusable blueprint for loading data.

Example:

```
from fastai.data.block import DataBlock
from fastai.vision.all import *
# Define a DataBlock
pets = DataBlock(
    blocks=(ImageBlock, CategoryBlock),
 # Input: Images, Output: Categories
    get_items=get_image_files,
 # How to get image file paths
    splitter=RandomSplitter(valid_pct=0.2),
 # Split data into train/validation sets
    get_y=parent_label,
```

```
    # Get labels from parent folder names
      item_tfms=Resize(224),
  # Resize images to 224x224
      batch_tfms=aug_transforms(mult=2.0)
   # Apply data augmentation
)
# Load the data
path = untar_data(URLs.PETS)/'images'
dls = pets.dataloaders(path)
```

Advantages of the DataBlock API

1. **Modularity**:
    a. Components like blocks, get_items, and splitter can be mixed and matched to suit different datasets.
2. **Reusability**:
    a. DataBlocks can be reused across multiple projects with similar data formats.
3. **Flexibility**:
    a. Customize every stage of the data pipeline for complex workflows.
4. **Simplified Debugging**:
    a. Use methods like summary() to inspect each step of the DataBlock.

Example:

```
# Inspect the DataBlock
pets.summary(path)
```

Real-World Applications The DataBlock API is versatile and supports a wide range of applications:

- **Image Classification**: Preparing image datasets for training models like ResNet.
- **Text Analysis**: Tokenizing and processing text for sentiment analysis or classification.
- **Tabular Data**: Handling missing values and encoding categorical variables for tabular models.
- **Custom Datasets**: Creating pipelines for unique data types, such as multi-label classification or time-series data.

The DataBlock API's modular and declarative design makes it an essential

Chapter - 2 Loading and Preparing Datasets with Fastai

This chapter introduces the essentials of loading and preparing datasets using the Fastai library. Fastai simplifies handling diverse datasets and provides powerful utilities for transforming, augmenting, and splitting data. This foundation is crucial for training machine learning models effectively and efficiently.

Key Characteristics of Loading and Preparing Datasets with Fastai:

- **DataBlock API:** A flexible and powerful tool for building data pipelines.
- **Integrated Data Augmentation:** Provides methods for data augmentation to improve model generalization.
- **Seamless Handling of Common Tasks:** Simplifies tasks like data normalization, splitting, and labeling.
- **Support for Multiple Formats:** Works with images, text, tabular data, and more.
- **Visualization Tools:** Allows inspection of datasets and transformations.

Basic Rules for Loading and Preparing Datasets with Fastai:

1. **Understand the Data Structure:** Ensure the dataset's format matches the requirements of the Fastai pipeline.
2. **Define a DataBlock:** Use the DataBlock API to describe how to preprocess and load the data.
3. **Apply Data Transformations:** Normalize, augment, or process the data as needed.
4. **Split the Data:** Ensure an appropriate train-test split using methods like random splitting or stratified splitting.
5. **Inspect the Data:** Visualize the dataset to confirm correctness and quality.

Syntax Table:

SL No	Function	Syntax/Example	Description
1	Define a DataBlock	`DataBlock(blocks, get_x, get_y, splitter)`	Creates a pipeline for data loading and processing.
2	Load Data with Dataloaders	`dblock.dataloaders(path)`	Converts a DataBlock into Dataloaders for training.
3	Normalize Data	`Normalize.from_stats(mean, std)`	Normalizes data based on mean and standard deviation.
4	Visualize Data	`dls.show_batch()`	Displays a batch of data to inspect augmentations.
5	Transform Data	`Resize(224)`	Resizes images to a consistent dimension.

Syntax Explanation:

1. Define a DataBlock

What is Defining a DataBlock?
The DataBlock API allows users to define how data is processed and organized into a pipeline.

Syntax:
```
from fastai.data.block import DataBlock
from fastai.data.transforms import get_image_files,
parent_label

dblock = DataBlock(
    blocks=(ImageBlock, CategoryBlock),
    get_items=get_image_files,
    get_y=parent_label,
    splitter=RandomSplitter(valid_pct=0.2)
)
```

Detailed Explanation:
- **Purpose:** Specifies the steps for processing data, including loading,

splitting, and labeling.
- **Parameters:**
  - `blocks`: Defines the types of input and output (e.g., ImageBlock for images and CategoryBlock for labels).
  - `get_items`: Function to retrieve items (e.g., `get_image_files` fetches image paths).
  - `get_y`: Extracts labels (e.g., `parent_label` assigns labels based on parent folder names).
  - `splitter`: Splits the data into training and validation sets (e.g., RandomSplitter).
- **Output:** A DataBlock blueprint ready for conversion into Dataloaders.

Example:
```
path = untar_data(URLs.PETS) / 'images'
dblock = DataBlock(
    blocks=(ImageBlock, CategoryBlock),
    get_items=get_image_files,
    get_y=parent_label,
    splitter=RandomSplitter(valid_pct=0.2)
)
```
Example Explanation:
- **Dataset Location:** Downloads and extracts the Oxford Pets dataset.
- **Blocks:** Defines that inputs are images and labels are categories.
- **Get Items and Labels:** Uses `get_image_files` and `parent_label` to fetch image paths and assign labels.
- **Splitter:** Reserves 20% of the data for validation.

2. Load Data with Dataloaders

What is Loading Data with Dataloaders?
Converts a DataBlock blueprint into Dataloaders, which handle batching, shuffling, and feeding data into the model during training and validation.
Syntax:
```
dls = dblock.dataloaders(path)
```
Detailed Explanation:
- **Purpose:** Generates Dataloaders for efficiently feeding data into

the model.

- **Parameters:**
    - ○ `path`: Directory containing the dataset.
- **Output:** Two Dataloaders: one for training and one for validation.
- **Features:**
    - ○ Automatically applies specified transformations.
    - ○ Handles data batching and shuffling.
    - ○ Prepares data for augmentation or preprocessing.

Example:
```
dls = dblock.dataloaders(path)
```
Example Explanation:

- Converts the DataBlock into Dataloaders for training and validation.
- Handles data preparation tasks like batching and applying augmentations.
- Ensures efficient data feeding during the model training cycle.

3. Normalize Data
What is Normalizing Data?
Normalizing input data involves scaling pixel values to have a mean of 0 and a standard deviation of 1. This ensures consistency across the dataset, stabilizes training, and helps models converge faster.

Syntax:
```
from fastai.data.transforms import Normalize
normalize = Normalize.from_stats(mean, std)
dls.after_batch.add(normalize)
```

Detailed Explanation:

- **Purpose:** Standardizes image pixel values for uniform input across the model.
- **Parameters:**
    - ○ `mean`: Average pixel values (e.g., `[0.485, 0.456, 0.406]` for ImageNet).
    - ○ `std`: Standard deviation of pixel values (e.g., `[0.229, 0.224, 0.225]`).
- **Output:** Normalized images ready for processing by the model.

Example:

```
dls.after_batch.add(Normalize.from_stats([0.485, 0.456,
0.406], [0.229, 0.224, 0.225]))
```

Example Explanation:

- Applies normalization based on precomputed ImageNet statistics.
- Ensures all images are scaled consistently for optimal model performance.

4. Visualize Data

What is Visualizing Data?

Displays samples from the dataset to verify preprocessing and transformations.

Syntax:

```
dls.show_batch(max_n=9)
```

Detailed Explanation:

- **Purpose:** Provides a visual inspection of data augmentations, resizing, and labeling.
- **Parameters:**
    - max_n: Number of images to display in the grid.
- **Output:** A grid of images showing preprocessed samples.

Example:

```
dls.show_batch(max_n=9, figsize=(6, 6))
```

Example Explanation:

- Displays 9 images from the dataset with augmentations applied.
- Allows users to confirm correctness of preprocessing steps.

5. Transform Data

What is Transforming Data?

Applies transformations like resizing and data augmentation to prepare data for training.

Syntax:

```
from fastai.vision.augment import Resize
resize = Resize(224)
dls.after_item.add(resize)
```

Detailed Explanation:

- **Purpose:** Ensures all input data has consistent dimensions and applies augmentations to improve model generalization.
- **Parameters:**
  - 224: Target size for resizing (e.g., 224x224 pixels).
- **Output:** Resized and augmented data fed into the model.

Example:

```
dls.after_item.add(Resize(224))
```

Example Explanation:

- Resizes images to 224x224 pixels for compatibility with pre-trained models.
- Improves computational efficiency and ensures uniformity in data processing.

Real-Life Project:

Project Name: Classifying Dog and Cat Images
Project Goal: Train a model to classify images of dogs and cats using the Fastai library.
Code for This Project:

```
from fastai.vision.all import *

# Load dataset
path = untar_data(URLs.PETS) / 'images'

# Define DataBlock
dblock = DataBlock(
    blocks=(ImageBlock, CategoryBlock),
    get_items=get_image_files,
    get_y=parent_label,
    splitter=RandomSplitter(valid_pct=0.2),
    item_tfms=Resize(224),
    batch_tfms=aug_transforms()
)
# Create Dataloaders
dls = dblock.dataloaders(path)
```

```
# Visualize data
dls.show_batch(max_n=9, figsize=(6, 6))

# Train model
learn = cnn_learner(dls, resnet34, metrics=error_rate)
learn.fine_tune(2)

# Evaluate model
interp =
ClassificationInterpretation.from_learner(learn)
interp.plot_confusion_matrix()
interp.plot_top_losses(5, nrows=1)
```
Expected Output:
- Confusion Matrix showing classification results.
- Top losses with corresponding misclassified images.

Chapter - 3 Exploring Data Augmentation Techniques

Data augmentation is a crucial technique in machine learning that enhances model generalization by artificially increasing the diversity of training data. In this chapter, we explore various augmentation techniques provided by Fastai, focusing on their implementation and benefits. By leveraging these techniques, you can improve your model's robustness and accuracy.

Key Characteristics of Data Augmentation:

- **Increased Dataset Diversity:** Generates new variations of data by applying transformations.
- **Prevention of Overfitting:** Reduces model dependency on specific features by exposing it to varied inputs.
- **Support for Multiple Data Types:** Applies to images, text, and tabular data.
- **Built-in Transformations:** Fastai provides easy-to-use augmentation functions.
- **Custom Augmentations:** Allows users to create custom augmentation pipelines tailored to specific tasks.

Common Data Augmentation Techniques:

1. **Image Transformations:** Resizing, flipping, rotation, cropping, and color adjustments.
2. **Text Augmentation:** Synonym replacement, sentence reordering, and back translation.
3. **Tabular Data Augmentation:** Noise injection and feature scaling.
4. **Combining Augmentations:** Creates robust pipelines by chaining multiple techniques.

Syntax Table:

SL No	Technique	Syntax/Example	Description
1	Apply Basic Transformations	`Resize(224)`	Resizes images to a fixed dimension.
2	Flip Images Horizontally	`aug_transforms(do_ flip=True)`	Randomly flips images horizontally.
3	Apply Rotation	`aug_transforms(max _rotate=10)`	Rotates images within a specified angle range.
4	Adjust Brightness/Contrast	`aug_transforms(bri ghtness=0.2, contrast=0.2)`	Adjusts brightness and contrast levels.
5	Create Augmentation Pipeline	`Pipeline([Rotate() , Flip()])`	Chains multiple transformations together.

Syntax Explanation:

1. Apply Basic Transformations
What is Applying Basic Transformations?
Ensures all images have a uniform size, simplifying preprocessing and model compatibility.
Syntax:
```
from fastai.vision.augment import Resize
resize = Resize(224)
```
Detailed Explanation:
- **Purpose:** Standardizes image dimensions to a fixed size (e.g., 224x224 pixels).
- **Parameters:**
    - 224: Target size for both width and height.
- **Output:** Resized images ready for use in the model pipeline.

Example:
```
dls = dblock.dataloaders(path, item_tfms=Resize(224))
```
Example Explanation:
- Applies resizing as part of the item transformations (`item_tfms`)

in the Dataloaders.

- Ensures all input images have consistent dimensions, which is essential for models like ResNet.
- Prevents errors during training caused by mismatched input sizes.

2. Flip Images Horizontally

What is Flipping Images Horizontally?

Randomly flips images along the horizontal axis to introduce variation.

Syntax:

```
from fastai.vision.augment import aug_transforms
dls = dblock.dataloaders(path,
batch_tfms=aug_transforms(do_flip=True))
```

Detailed Explanation:

- **Purpose:** Simulates different viewpoints by flipping images horizontally.
- **Parameters:**
  - o do_flip=True: Enables random horizontal flipping.
- **Output:** Augmented images with flipped variations.

Example:

```
batch_tfms = aug_transforms(do_flip=True)
dls = dblock.dataloaders(path, batch_tfms=batch_tfms)
```

Example Explanation:

- Flipping introduces variations, especially useful for datasets like animals or vehicles, where horizontal orientation isn't critical.
- Helps prevent overfitting by making the model less reliant on specific orientations.

3. Apply Rotation

What is Applying Rotation?

Rotates images within a specified angle range to simulate different perspectives.

Syntax:

- from fastai.vision.augment import aug_transforms
  dls = dblock.dataloaders(path, **Purpose:** Introduces variability by tilting images to mimic real-world scenarios, such as slightly rotated photos.

- **Parameters:**
  - max_rotate=10: Specifies the maximum rotation angle (in degrees).
- **Output:** Images rotated within the defined range.

Example:
```
batch_tfms = aug_transforms(max_rotate=10)
dls = dblock.dataloaders(path, batch_tfms=batch_tfms)
```
Example Explanation:
- Rotation is particularly useful for datasets with varying orientations, like scanned documents or wildlife photos.
- Enhances the model's ability to recognize objects at different angles.

4. Adjust Brightness/Contrast

What is Adjusting Brightness and Contrast?
Alters the brightness and contrast levels of images to simulate different lighting conditions.

Syntax:
```
from fastai.vision.augment import aug_transforms
dls = dblock.dataloaders(path,
batch_tfms=aug_transforms(brightness=0.2,
contrast=0.2))
```
Detailed Explanation:
- **Purpose:** Mimics real-world lighting variations to improve model adaptability.
- **Parameters:**
  - brightness=0.2: Adjusts brightness within the range (-0.2, 0.2).
  - contrast=0.2: Adjusts contrast within the range (-0.2, 0.2).
- **Output:** Brightness- and contrast-adjusted images.

Example:
```
batch_tfms = aug_transforms(brightness=0.2,
contrast=0.2)
dls = dblock.dataloaders(path, batch_tfms=batch_tfms)
```
Example Explanation:

- Adjustments allow the model to generalize better to images captured under varying light conditions, such as indoor and outdoor settings.
- Particularly beneficial for datasets with diverse lighting environments.

5. Create Augmentation Pipeline
What is Creating an Augmentation Pipeline?
Combines multiple augmentation techniques into a single pipeline for enhanced data diversity.
Syntax:
```
from fastai.vision.augment import aug_transforms
dls = dblock.dataloaders(path,
batch_tfms=aug_transforms(do_flip=True, max_rotate=10,
brightness=0.2, contrast=0.2))
```
Detailed Explanation:
- **Purpose:** Chains several augmentation techniques to create a comprehensive pipeline, providing robust data variations.
- **Parameters:**
  - Includes flipping, rotation, brightness, and contrast adjustments.
- **Output:** Augmented images with multiple transformations applied.

Example:
```
batch_tfms = aug_transforms(do_flip=True,
max_rotate=10, brightness=0.2, contrast=0.2)
dls = dblock.dataloaders(path, batch_tfms=batch_tfms)
```
Example Explanation:
- Each augmentation technique is applied in sequence, ensuring a variety of transformations.
- Creates a highly diverse dataset, improving the model's robustness and reducing overfitting.
- Useful in complex tasks like object detection or fine-grained image classification.

Real-Life Project:

Project Name: Enhancing Image Classification with Data Augmentation

Project Goal:

Demonstrate the impact of data augmentation on model performance by training a robust image classifier.

Code for This Project:

```python
from fastai.vision.all import *
# Load dataset
path = untar_data(URLs.PETS) / 'images'
# Define DataBlock
dblock = DataBlock(
    blocks=(ImageBlock, CategoryBlock),
    get_items=get_image_files,
    get_y=parent_label,
    splitter=RandomSplitter(valid_pct=0.2),
    item_tfms=Resize(224),
    batch_tfms=aug_transforms(
        do_flip=True, max_rotate=10, brightness=0.2,
contrast=0.2
    )
)
# Create Dataloaders
dls = dblock.dataloaders(path)
# Visualize augmented data
dls.show_batch(max_n=9, figsize=(6, 6))
# Train model
learn = cnn_learner(dls, resnet34, metrics=error_rate)
learn.fine_tune(2)
# Evaluate model
interp =
ClassificationInterpretation.from_learner(learn)
interp.plot_confusion_matrix()
interp.plot_top_losses(5, nrows=1)
```

Expected Output:

- Visualization of augmented data samples.
- Confusion matrix showing classification performance.
- Top misclassified examples with corresponding losses.

Chapter - 4 Working with Learner Objects in Fastai

The Learner object is the central component in Fastai for model training, evaluation, and interpretation. This chapter explores how to create, configure, and utilize Learner objects effectively. By mastering the Learner, you can streamline the process of building machine learning models, track performance, and extract insights.

Key Characteristics of Learner Objects:

- **Model Training:** Simplifies the training process with built-in functions like fit and fine_tune.
- **Metrics Tracking:** Tracks key performance metrics during training and validation.
- **Callback Support:** Allows custom behavior during training via callbacks.
- **Integrated Interpretation Tools:** Provides methods for visualizing and interpreting model results.
- **Flexibility:** Supports a wide range of architectures and tasks, including vision, text, and tabular data.

Basic Rules for Working with Learner Objects:

1. **Define the Data:** Create Dataloaders with preprocessed data.
2. **Select a Model Architecture:** Choose an architecture suitable for the task, such as resnet34 for image classification.
3. **Specify Metrics:** Add metrics to track during training (e.g., accuracy or error_rate).
4. **Train the Model:** Use methods like fit or fine_tune for training.
5. **Evaluate and Interpret Results:** Utilize built-in tools for analysis and debugging.

Syntax Table:

SL No	Function	Syntax/Example	Description
1	Create a Learner	`cnn_learner(dls, resnet34, metrics=accuracy)`	Initializes a Learner object.
2	Train the Model	`learn.fit(n_epochs)`	Trains the model for a specified number of epochs.
3	Fine-Tune Pretrained Model	`learn.fine_tune(n_epochs)`	Fine-tunes a model pretrained on ImageNet.
4	Interpret Results	`ClassificationInterpretation.from_learner(learn)`	Provides tools for analyzing predictions.
5	Save/Load Model Weights	`learn.save('model_name')` / `learn.load('model_name')`	Saves or loads model weights.

Syntax Explanation:

1. Create a Learner

What is Creating a Learner?

The Learner object serves as an all-in-one framework that integrates essential components of machine learning: the model, training and validation data, optimization algorithm, loss function, and evaluation metrics. It streamlines the entire workflow, allowing for seamless training, validation, and interpretation within a unified interface.

Syntax:

```
from fastai.vision.all import *
learn = cnn_learner(dls, resnet34, metrics=accuracy)
```

Detailed Explanation:

- **Purpose:** Initializes a Learner object for training and evaluation.
- **Parameters:**
    - dls: Dataloaders containing training and validation data.

- o   resnet34: Model architecture (e.g., ResNet with 34 layers).
- o   metrics: A list of metrics to monitor during training (e.g., accuracy).
- **Output:** A configured Learner object ready for training.

Example:

```
learn = cnn_learner(dls, resnet34, metrics=[error_rate, accuracy])
```

Example Explanation:

- Combines the ResNet-34 architecture with data from dls.
- Tracks both error_rate and accuracy metrics during training.
- Allows quick evaluation of model performance after training.

2. Train the Model

What is Training the Model?

Uses the fit method to iteratively train the model by passing batches of data through it for a specified number of epochs. During this process, the model's parameters are updated based on the computed gradients of the loss function, aiming to minimize the difference between predicted and actual outputs.

Syntax:

```
learn.fit(n_epochs)
```

Detailed Explanation:

- **Purpose:** Optimizes model parameters to minimize the loss function.
- **Parameters:**
  - o   n_epochs: Number of times the model iterates over the entire dataset.
- **Output:**
  - o   Logs of training and validation loss for each epoch.
  - o   Metric values (e.g., accuracy or error rate) to track performance.

Example:

```
learn.fit(5)
```

Example Explanation:
- Trains the model for 5 epochs, updating weights after each batch.
- Provides feedback on progress by printing training and validation loss after each epoch.
- Useful for assessing convergence and adjusting training duration if necessary.

3. Fine-Tune Pretrained Model
What is Fine-Tuning a Pretrained Model?

Leverages the knowledge acquired by a model trained on a large and diverse dataset (e.g., ImageNet) to effectively handle a new, more specific task with limited data. This process involves fine-tuning the model's parameters, allowing it to adapt and generalize to the new dataset while retaining valuable feature representations from its pretraining.

Syntax:
```
learn.fine_tune(n_epochs)
```

Detailed Explanation:
- **Purpose:** Fine-tunes the model's parameters to align with the new dataset while leveraging pretrained knowledge.
- **Parameters:**
  - n_epochs: Number of epochs for fine-tuning.
- **Output:** Training and validation metrics for each epoch.
- **How it Works:**
  - Initially freezes the base layers and trains only the head.
  - Unfreezes all layers for subsequent fine-tuning, allowing adjustments to pretrained features.

Example:
```
learn.fine_tune(3)
```
Example Explanation:
- Fine-tunes the model for 3 epochs, typically achieving faster convergence compared to training from scratch.
- Uses pretrained weights to improve accuracy on smaller datasets by leveraging features learned on a larger dataset like ImageNet.

4. Interpret Results

What is Interpreting Results?

Examines the model's predictions to uncover patterns of errors and specific areas where it may struggle. This analysis helps to identify frequently misclassified classes, outlier data points, and potential weaknesses in preprocessing or feature representation. Such insights are crucial for refining the model, improving data quality, or adjusting hyperparameters to enhance performance.

Syntax:

```
from fastai.vision.all import
ClassificationInterpretation
interp =
ClassificationInterpretation.from_learner(learn)
interp.plot_confusion_matrix()
interp.plot_top_losses(5, nrows=1)
```

Detailed Explanation:

- **Purpose:** Provides tools for error analysis and visualization.
- **Key Methods:**
  - `plot_confusion_matrix()`: Displays a confusion matrix to analyze classification performance by showing true vs. predicted classes.
  - `plot_top_losses(n, nrows)`: Visualizes the most significant errors made by the model.
- **Output:**
  - A confusion matrix helps identify which classes are often misclassified.
  - Images with top losses highlight areas where the model struggled.

Example:

```
interp =
ClassificationInterpretation.from_learner(learn)
interp.plot_confusion_matrix()
interp.plot_top_losses(3, nrows=1)
```

Example Explanation:

- The confusion matrix reveals the distribution of correct and incorrect predictions.
- Top loss examples allow targeted inspection of misclassified data,

aiding in debugging and improving preprocessing.

5. Save/Load Model Weights

What is Saving and Loading Model Weights?
Saves the current state of the model, including all learned parameters and configurations, into a file, enabling reuse or continuation of training at a later time. Reloading the model restores it exactly as it was saved, ensuring consistency in results and eliminating the need for retraining from scratch.

Syntax:
```
learn.save('model_name')
learn.load('model_name')
```
Detailed Explanation:
- **Purpose:** Ensures model progress is not lost and allows reuse of trained models.
- **Parameters:**
  - model_name: Name for the saved model file.
- **Output:**
  - save: Creates a file storing model parameters.
  - load: Restores model parameters from a file.

Example:
```
learn.save('stage-1')
learn.load('stage-1')
```
Example Explanation:
- Saves the model state after the first training stage.
- Reloads the same state to continue training or evaluate performance later.
- Ensures reproducibility and saves time by avoiding retraining from scratch.

Real-Life Project:
Project Name: Image Classification with Learner Objects
Project Goal: Train a ResNet-based classifier to distinguish between dogs and cats using the Fastai Learner.

Code for This Project:

```python
from fastai.vision.all import *
# Load dataset
path = untar_data(URLs.PETS) / 'images'
# Define DataBlock
dblock = DataBlock(
    blocks=(ImageBlock, CategoryBlock),
    get_items=get_image_files,
    get_y=parent_label,
    splitter=RandomSplitter(valid_pct=0.2),
    item_tfms=Resize(224),
    batch_tfms=aug_transforms()
)
# Create Dataloaders
dls = dblock.dataloaders(path)
# Initialize Learner
learn = cnn_learner(dls, resnet34, metrics=[error_rate, accuracy])

# Fine-tune the model
learn.fine_tune(3)

# Interpret results
interp = ClassificationInterpretation.from_learner(learn)
interp.plot_confusion_matrix()
interp.plot_top_losses(5, nrows=1)

# Save and load model
learn.save('dog-cat-classifier')
learn.load('dog-cat-classifier')
```

Expected Output:

- Visualization of model performance through confusion matrix and top losses.
- Saved model ready for reuse or deployment.

Chapter - 5 Customizing Training Loops in Fastai

Customizing training loops allows users to tailor the training process for unique requirements, beyond the standard workflows provided by Fastai's Learner object. This chapter explores how to modify and extend training loops, leveraging callbacks and custom logic to implement advanced features such as dynamic learning rates, early stopping, and custom metrics.

Key Characteristics of Customizing Training Loops:

- **Flexibility:** Supports tailored workflows for specialized tasks.
- **Callback Integration:** Provides hooks for injecting custom logic at specific points in the training loop.
- **Dynamic Adjustments:** Enables dynamic changes to learning rates, losses, or other parameters during training.
- **Comprehensive Access:** Grants full access to the training loop's components, including model, optimizer, and data.
- **Error Handling and Debugging:** Facilitates advanced monitoring and control for robust experimentation.

Basic Rules for Customizing Training Loops:

1. **Understand the Training Loop:** Familiarize yourself with the core phases of Fastai's training loop (e.g., data loading, forward pass, loss computation, backward pass, and optimization).
2. **Use Callbacks:** Leverage Fastai's callback system to inject logic into the training process.
3. **Monitor Metrics and Losses:** Track relevant metrics and losses to validate your customizations.
4. **Optimize Performance:** Ensure that customizations do not degrade model performance or training efficiency.
5. **Test Incrementally:** Validate each change with a subset of data before applying it to the full dataset.

Syntax Table:

SL No	Function	Syntax/Example	Description
1	Create a Custom Callback	`class CustomCallback(Callback):`	Defines a new callback to modify training logic.
2	Add Callback to Learner	`learn.add_cb(CustomCallback())`	Adds a custom callback to the Learner.
3	Access Training Loop Attributes	`self.learn.loss_func`	Accesses components like loss function, model, etc.
4	Implement Early Stopping	`if metric_value > threshold: self.learn.stop`	Stops training when a condition is met.
5	Adjust Learning Rate	`self.learn.opt.set_hyper('lr', new_lr)`	Dynamically updates the learning rate.

Syntax Explanation:

1. Create a Custom Callback

What is Creating a Custom Callback?

A custom callback allows users to inject custom logic into specific stages of the training process, such as before or after a batch is processed.

Syntax:

```
from fastai.callback.core import Callback
class CustomCallback(Callback):
    def before_epoch(self):
        print("Starting epoch", self.epoch)

    def after_batch(self):
        print("Completed batch", self.iter)
```

Detailed Explanation:

- **Purpose:** Adds custom behavior at predefined points in the training loop.
- **Key Methods:**

- o before_epoch: Executes logic before each epoch starts.
- o after_batch: Executes logic after processing each batch.
- **Output:** Prints messages or performs custom operations at defined stages.

Example:

```
class PrintBatchCallback(Callback):
    def after_batch(self):
        print(f"Batch {self.iter} processed with loss
{self.learn.loss.item()}")
```

Example Explanation:
- Logs the loss value after every batch is processed.
- Useful for debugging or monitoring training progress in real-time.

2. Add Callback to Learner
What is Adding a Callback to the Learner?
Integrates the custom callback into the training process by attaching it to the Learner object.

Syntax:

```
learn.add_cb(CustomCallback())
```

Detailed Explanation:
- **Purpose:** Enables the Learner to execute the logic defined in the custom callback.
- **Parameters:**
  - o CustomCallback(): An instance of the custom callback class.
- **Output:** Executes the callback's methods at the appropriate stages during training.

Example:

```
learn = cnn_learner(dls, resnet34, metrics=accuracy)
learn.add_cb(PrintBatchCallback())
learn.fit(1)
```

Example Explanation:
- Integrates PrintBatchCallback into the training loop.
- Logs batch-level loss values during the single-epoch training run.

3. Access Training Loop Attributes
What is Accessing Training Loop Attributes?
Allows callbacks to interact with key components of the training loop, such as the model, optimizer, and metrics.
Syntax:
```
self.learn.loss_func
self.learn.model
self.learn.opt
```
Detailed Explanation:
- **Purpose:** Enables custom callbacks to read or modify training loop attributes.
- **Common Attributes:**
    - `self.learn.loss_func`: The loss function used during training.
    - `self.learn.model`: The model being trained.
    - `self.learn.opt`: The optimizer managing parameter updates.
- **Output:** Provides access to training loop components for advanced customizations.

Example:
```
class MonitorGradientsCallback(Callback):
    def after_backward(self):
        print(f"Gradient Norm:
{self.learn.model[0].weight.grad.norm()}")
```
Example Explanation:
- Logs the gradient norm of the first layer after each backward pass.
- Helps monitor optimization dynamics and detect potential issues like vanishing or exploding gradients.

4. Implement Early Stopping
What is Early Stopping?
Stops training when a specified condition, such as no improvement in validation loss, is met.
Syntax:
```
if metric_value > threshold:
    self.learn.stop
```

Detailed Explanation:

- **Purpose:** Prevents overfitting by halting training once performance ceases to improve.
- **How it Works:**
    - Monitors a validation metric (e.g., accuracy or loss).
    - Compares the metric to a predefined threshold.
    - Stops training when the condition is satisfied.
- **Output:** Ends the training loop gracefully when the stopping criterion is met.

Example:

```python
class EarlyStoppingCallback(Callback):
    def __init__(self, monitor='valid_loss',
patience=3):
        self.monitor = monitor
        self.patience = patience
        self.best_value = float('inf')
        self.counter = 0
    def after_epoch(self):
        current = self.learn.recorder.values[-1][0]
        if current < self.best_value:
            self.best_value = current
            self.counter = 0
        else:
            self.counter += 1
            if self.counter >= self.patience:
                print("Early stopping triggered")
                self.learn.stop = True
```

Example Explanation:

- Tracks validation loss over epochs.
- Stops training after 3 consecutive epochs without improvement.
- Prevents wasting resources on unproductive training.

5. Adjust Learning Rate

What is Adjusting the Learning Rate?

Dynamically modifies the learning rate during training to improve convergence.

Syntax:
```
self.learn.opt.set_hyper('lr', new_lr)
```
Detailed Explanation:
- **Purpose:** Adapts the learning rate based on training progress, often leading to faster and more stable convergence.
- **Parameters:**
    - new_lr: The updated learning rate value.
- **Output:** Updates the optimizer with the new learning rate.

Example:
```
class DynamicLRCallback(Callback):
    def after_epoch(self):
        new_lr = self.learn.opt.hypers[0]['lr'] * 0.9
        self.learn.opt.set_hyper('lr', new_lr)
        print(f"Learning rate adjusted to {new_lr}")
```
Example Explanation:
- Reduces the learning rate by 10% after each epoch.
- Helps the model fine-tune its weights as training progresses.

Real-Life Project:

Project Name: Custom Training for Image Classification
Project Goal:
Demonstrate the use of callbacks and custom training logic to implement dynamic learning rate adjustment and early stopping for an image classification task.
Code for This Project:
```
from fastai.vision.all import *

# Load dataset
path = untar_data(URLs.PETS) / 'images'

# Define DataBlock
dblock = DataBlock(
    blocks=(ImageBlock, CategoryBlock),
    get_items=get_image_files,
    get_y=parent_label,
    splitter=RandomSplitter(valid_pct=0.2),
```

```
    item_tfms=Resize(224),
    batch_tfms=aug_transforms()
)
# Create Dataloaders
dls = dblock.dataloaders(path)

# Initialize Learner
learn = cnn_learner(dls, resnet34, metrics=accuracy)

# Add Custom Callbacks
learn.add_cb(DynamicLRCallback())
learn.add_cb(EarlyStoppingCallback(monitor='valid_loss'
, patience=3))

# Train the model
learn.fit(10)
```

Expected Output:

- Dynamic adjustment of learning rates during training.
- Early stopping triggered if validation loss stops improving.
- Logs showing batch-level and epoch-level training details.

Chapter – 6 Understanding Metrics and Loss Functions in Fastai

Metrics and loss functions are essential components of machine learning workflows, as they evaluate model performance and guide optimization. In this chapter, we explore the differences between metrics and loss functions, discuss common examples, and demonstrate how to implement and customize them in Fastai.

Key Characteristics of Metrics and Loss Functions:

- **Metrics:**
    - Evaluate model performance during training and validation.
    - Focus on human-understandable measures like accuracy, precision, or F1-score.
    - Do not influence model optimization directly.
- **Loss Functions:**
    - Guide model optimization by computing the error between predictions and ground truth.
    - Must be differentiable for gradient-based optimization methods.
    - Examples include cross-entropy loss, mean squared error, and binary cross-entropy.

Basic Rules for Metrics and Loss Functions in Fastai:

1. **Select Appropriate Metrics:** Match metrics to the task (e.g., accuracy for classification, RMSE for regression).
2. **Choose a Compatible Loss Function:** Ensure the loss function aligns with the output activation and problem type (e.g., `CrossEntropyLoss` for classification).
3. **Monitor Metrics:** Track metrics during training to evaluate progress and performance.
4. **Understand Metric-Loss Differences:** Metrics are for evaluation, while loss functions are for optimization.
5. **Customize When Necessary:** Implement custom metrics or loss functions if prebuilt ones are insufficient.

Syntax Table:

SL No	Function	Syntax/Example	Description
1	Add Metrics to Learner	`cnn_learner(dls, resnet34, metrics=accuracy)`	Monitors accuracy during training.
2	Specify Loss Function	`Learner(dls, model, loss_func=CrossEntrop yLossFlat())`	Defines the loss function for optimization.
3	Implement Custom Metric	`def custom_metric(preds, targs):`	Defines a custom evaluation metric.
4	Access Recorded Metrics	`learn.recorder.values`	Retrieves training and validation metrics.
5	Customize Loss Function	`class CustomLoss(Module):`	Implements a new loss function.

Syntax Explanation:

1. Add Metrics to Learner
What is Adding Metrics to Learner?
Metrics evaluate the model's performance on validation data, providing insights during training.
Syntax:
```
from fastai.vision.all import *
learn = cnn_learner(dls, resnet34, metrics=accuracy)
```
Detailed Explanation:
- **Purpose:** Tracks evaluation metrics like accuracy during training.
- **Parameters:**
    - `metrics`: A list of predefined or custom metrics.
- **Output:** Logs metric values after each epoch.
Example:
```
learn = cnn_learner(dls, resnet34, metrics=[accuracy, error_rate])
```
Example Explanation:

- Tracks both `accuracy` and `error_rate` during training.
- Helps assess whether the model is improving over epochs.

2. Specify Loss Function
What is Specifying a Loss Function?
Defines the function that calculates the error between predictions and actual values, guiding optimization.
Syntax:
```
from fastai.vision.all import *
learn = Learner(dls, model,
loss_func=CrossEntropyLossFlat())
```
Detailed Explanation:
- **Purpose:** Specifies how the model's performance is measured during optimization.
- **Parameters:**
  - `loss_func`: The loss function to compute the error.
- **Output:** Trains the model using the specified loss function.

Example:
```
learn = Learner(dls, model,
loss_func=CrossEntropyLossFlat(), metrics=accuracy)
```
Example Explanation:
- Uses cross-entropy loss, a standard choice for multi-class classification.
- Tracks accuracy to evaluate model performance during training.

3. Implement Custom Metric
What is a Custom Metric?
Custom metrics allow users to define evaluation measures not available in Fastai's predefined list.
Syntax:
```
def custom_metric(preds, targs):
    return (preds.argmax(dim=-1) ==
targs).float().mean()
```
Detailed Explanation:
- **Purpose:** Evaluates specific aspects of model performance.
- **Parameters:**

- o   preds: Model predictions.
- o   targs: Ground truth labels.
- **Output:** Returns a scalar metric value (e.g., accuracy, F1-score).

Example:

```
def precision_metric(preds, targs):
    tp = ((preds.argmax(dim=-1) == 1) & (targs ==
1)).sum()
    fp = ((preds.argmax(dim=-1) == 1) & (targs ==
0)).sum()
    return tp / (tp + fp + 1e-8)
```

Example Explanation:

- Computes precision by counting true positives (tp) and false positives (fp).
- Helps evaluate model performance on imbalanced datasets.

4. Access Recorded Metrics

What is Accessing Recorded Metrics?

Retrieves metric values logged during training for further analysis.

Syntax:

```
learn.recorder.values
```

Detailed Explanation:

- **Purpose:** Analyzes training and validation metrics after training.
- **Output:** A list of recorded metric values for each epoch.

Example:

```
metrics = learn.recorder.values
print("Validation Accuracy:", metrics[-1][2])
```

Example Explanation:

- Retrieves the accuracy value for the last epoch.
- Useful for plotting or comparing model performance.

5. Customize Loss Function

What is a Custom Loss Function?

Defines a new loss function tailored to specific requirements of the task.

Syntax:

```
from torch.nn import Module
class CustomLoss(Module):
```

```
def forward(self, preds, targs):
    return (preds - targs).abs().mean()
```

Detailed Explanation:

- **Purpose:** Implements task-specific error calculations.
- **Parameters:**
  - preds: Model predictions.
  - targs: Ground truth labels.
- **Output:** Scalar loss value for backpropagation.

Example:
```
learn = Learner(dls, model, loss_func=CustomLoss(),
metrics=accuracy)
```

Example Explanation:

- Uses CustomLoss to compute mean absolute error.
- Tracks accuracy for evaluation alongside custom loss optimization.

Real-Life Project:

Project Name: Evaluating Metrics and Loss for Multi-Class Classification

Project Goal:

Train a multi-class classifier with a custom loss function and evaluate it using precision and recall metrics.

Code for This Project:
```
from fastai.vision.all import *
# Load dataset
path = untar_data(URLs.PETS) / 'images'
# Define DataBlock
dblock = DataBlock(
    blocks=(ImageBlock, CategoryBlock),
    get_items=get_image_files,
    get_y=parent_label,
    splitter=RandomSplitter(valid_pct=0.2),
    item_tfms=Resize(224),
    batch_tfms=aug_transforms()
)
# Create Dataloaders
dls = dblock.dataloaders(path)

# Define Custom Metric
```

```python
def f1_metric(preds, targs):
    tp = ((preds.argmax(dim=-1) == targs) & (targs ==
1)).sum()
    fp = ((preds.argmax(dim=-1) != targs) & (targs ==
0)).sum()
    fn = ((preds.argmax(dim=-1) != targs) & (targs ==
1)).sum()
    return 2 * tp / (2 * tp + fp + fn + 1e-8)
# Initialize Learner
learn = cnn_learner(dls, resnet34,
loss_func=CrossEntropyLossFlat(), metrics=[accuracy,
f1_metric])

# Train the model
learn.fine_tune(3)

# Access metrics
metrics = learn.recorder.values
print("Final Validation Accuracy:", metrics[-1][1])
```
Expected Output:
- Metrics like accuracy and F1-score after each epoch.
- Final validation accuracy for performance evaluation.

Chapter -6 Image Classification with Fastai

Image classification is one of the most fundamental tasks in computer vision, where the goal is to assign a label to an image. In this chapter, we explore how to perform image classification using the Fastai library. We cover dataset preparation, model training, evaluation, and techniques to improve classification accuracy.

Key Characteristics of Image Classification with Fastai:

- **DataBlock API:** Simplifies the process of preparing datasets.
- **Pretrained Models:** Leverages pretrained models like ResNet for transfer learning.
- **Integrated Augmentations:** Enhances model generalization with built-in data augmentation.
- **Metrics and Loss Tracking:** Monitors performance during training.
- **Interpretation Tools:** Provides insights into model predictions and errors.

Basic Steps for Image Classification:

1. **Load and Prepare Data:** Use the DataBlock API to preprocess and organize data.
2. **Initialize the Learner:** Select a pretrained model and metrics.
3. **Train the Model:** Use methods like fit or fine_tune to train the classifier.
4. **Evaluate Results:** Analyze performance using metrics and interpretation tools.
5. **Optimize and Deploy:** Apply techniques like learning rate tuning or model pruning for deployment.

Syntax Table:

SL No	Function	Syntax/Example	Description
1	Load Dataset	`untar_data(URLs.PETS)`	Downloads and extracts a dataset.
2	Create DataBlock	`DataBlock(blocks, get_items, splitter, ...)`	Defines the dataset pipeline.
3	Create Dataloaders	`dblock.dataloaders(path)`	Converts a DataBlock into Dataloaders.
4	Train with Learner	`cnn_learner(dls, resnet34, metrics)`	Initializes and trains a model.
5	Interpret Results	`ClassificationInterpretation.from_learner()`	Provides tools for analyzing predictions.

Syntax Explanation:

1. Load Dataset

What is Loading a Dataset?

Fastai provides utilities to download and extract datasets directly from common sources.

Syntax:

```
from fastai.vision.all import *
path = untar_data(URLs.PETS)
```

Detailed Explanation:

- **Purpose:** Prepares a dataset for training and validation.
- **Parameters:**
    - URLs.PETS: A predefined URL for the Oxford-IIIT Pet Dataset.
- **Output:** Returns the path to the downloaded dataset.

Example:

```
path = untar_data(URLs.PETS) / 'images'
print(path)
```

Example Explanation:

- Downloads the Oxford Pets dataset and extracts it to the local file system.
- Returns the directory path where the dataset is stored.

2. Create DataBlock
What is Creating a DataBlock?
The DataBlock API defines how data is loaded, split, labeled, and transformed.
Syntax:
```
dblock = DataBlock(
    blocks=(ImageBlock, CategoryBlock),
    get_items=get_image_files,
    get_y=parent_label,
    splitter=RandomSplitter(valid_pct=0.2),
    item_tfms=Resize(224),
    batch_tfms=aug_transforms()
)
```
Detailed Explanation:
- **Purpose:** Specifies the dataset structure and preprocessing steps.
- **Parameters:**
  - blocks: Defines input-output types (e.g., images and categories).
  - get_items: Function to retrieve file paths (e.g., get_image_files).
  - get_y: Function to extract labels (e.g., parent_label).
  - splitter: Splits the dataset into training and validation sets.
  - item_tfms: Applies transformations like resizing to individual items.
  - batch_tfms: Adds batch-level augmentations like flipping or rotation.
- **Output:** A blueprint for creating Dataloaders.

Example:
```
dblock = DataBlock(
    blocks=(ImageBlock, CategoryBlock),
    get_items=get_image_files,
```

```
    get_y=parent_label,
    splitter=RandomSplitter(valid_pct=0.2)
)
```

Example Explanation:

- Defines an image classification pipeline.
- Uses parent directory names for labels and reserves 20% of the data for validation.

3. Create Dataloaders

What are Dataloaders?

Dataloaders handle data batching, shuffling, and preprocessing during training.

Syntax:

```
dls = dblock.dataloaders(path)
```

Detailed Explanation:

- **Purpose:** Converts the DataBlock into Dataloaders for training.
- **Parameters:**
  - o path: Path to the dataset directory.
- **Output:** Two Dataloaders (training and validation).

Example:

```
dls = dblock.dataloaders(path)
dls.show_batch(max_n=9, figsize=(6, 6))
```

Example Explanation:

- Visualizes a batch of images and their corresponding labels.
- Ensures the dataset pipeline is functioning correctly.

4. Train with Learner

What is Training with Learner?

The Learner object simplifies the training process by integrating data, model, optimizer, and metrics.

Syntax:

```
learn = cnn_learner(dls, resnet34, metrics=accuracy)
learn.fine_tune(3)
```

Detailed Explanation:

- **Purpose:** Trains a model using transfer learning and predefined metrics.
- **Parameters:**
    - dls: Dataloaders for training and validation.
    - resnet34: Pretrained ResNet-34 architecture.
    - metrics: List of metrics to track (e.g., accuracy).
- **Output:** Trained model with logged metrics.

Example:
```
learn = cnn_learner(dls, resnet34, metrics=accuracy)
learn.fine_tune(5)
```
Example Explanation:
- Fine-tunes a ResNet-34 model for 5 epochs.
- Tracks validation accuracy after each epoch.

5. Interpret Results

What is Interpreting Results?

Fastai provides tools to analyze predictions, errors, and overall performance.

Syntax:
```
interp = ClassificationInterpretation.from_learner(learn)
interp.plot_confusion_matrix()
interp.plot_top_losses(5, nrows=1)
```

Detailed Explanation:
- **Purpose:** Visualizes areas where the model excels or struggles.
- **Key Methods:**
    - plot_confusion_matrix: Displays true vs. predicted labels.
    - plot_top_losses: Highlights the most significant errors.
- **Output:** Graphical summaries for error analysis.

Example:
```
interp = ClassificationInterpretation.from_learner(learn)
interp.plot_confusion_matrix()
interp.plot_top_losses(3, nrows=1)
```

Example Explanation:
- The confusion matrix shows the distribution of correct and incorrect predictions.
- Top losses reveal samples where the model struggled, aiding debugging.

Real-Life Project:

Project Name: Classifying Dogs and Cats with ResNet

Project Goal: Build and evaluate a model to classify images of dogs and cats.

Code for This Project:

```
from fastai.vision.all import *
# Load dataset
path = untar_data(URLs.PETS) / 'images'
# Define DataBlock
dblock = DataBlock(
    blocks=(ImageBlock, CategoryBlock),
    get_items=get_image_files,
    get_y=parent_label,
    splitter=RandomSplitter(valid_pct=0.2),
    item_tfms=Resize(224),
    batch_tfms=aug_transforms()
)
# Create Dataloaders
dls = dblock.dataloaders(path)
# Initialize Learner
learn = cnn_learner(dls, resnet34, metrics=accuracy)
# Train the model
learn.fine_tune(3)
# Interpret results
interp =
ClassificationInterpretation.from_learner(learn)
interp.plot_confusion_matrix()
interp.plot_top_losses(5, nrows=1)
```

Expected Output:
- Visualization of training progress and metrics.
- Confusion matrix and top losses for performance analysis.
- Trained model ready for deployment.

Chapter - 7 Object Detection with Fastai

Object detection combines image classification and localization, enabling models to identify and locate multiple objects within an image. This chapter explores how to implement object detection using Fastai, leveraging its flexible DataBlock API, pretrained models, and customization capabilities.

Key Characteristics of Object Detection with Fastai:

- **Multi-task Learning:** Simultaneously predicts class labels and bounding box coordinates.
- **Data Augmentation:** Provides transformations specific to object detection tasks.
- **Pretrained Backbones:** Uses pretrained CNN architectures for feature extraction.
- **Customizable Pipelines:** Adapts easily to various object detection datasets.
- **Interpretation Tools:** Visualizes predictions and evaluates detection performance.

Basic Steps for Object Detection:

1. **Prepare the Dataset:** Organize images and annotations into a suitable format.
2. **Define the DataBlock:** Specify inputs, labels, and transformations.
3. **Initialize the Learner:** Choose a model architecture and loss function.
4. **Train the Model:** Optimize using `fit` or `fine_tune` methods.
5. **Evaluate Results:** Visualize and analyze detection performance.

Syntax Table:

SL No	Function	Syntax/Example	Description
1	Load and Parse Dataset	`load_data(path)`	Loads images and annotations.
2	Create DataBlock for Detection	`DataBlock(blocks, get_items, get_y, splitter)`	Defines the data pipeline for object detection.
3	Apply	`Resize` and	Preprocesses images

	Transformatio ns	`aug_transforms()`	and augments data.
4	Train the Model	`learn.fit(n_epochs )`	Optimizes the detection model.
5	Visualize Predictions	`learn.show_results ()`	Displays predicted bounding boxes and labels.

Syntax Explanation:

1. Load and Parse Dataset

What is Loading and Parsing a Dataset?

Organizes the dataset into images and corresponding bounding box annotations.

Syntax:

```
from fastai.vision.all import *
annotations = pd.read_csv('annotations.csv')
path = Path('images')
```

Detailed Explanation:

- **Purpose:** Prepares data for object detection tasks.
- **Input:**
  - `annotations.csv`: Contains image paths, bounding box coordinates, and class labels.
  - `images`: Directory containing the image files.
- **Output:** Dataframe or dictionary pairing images with annotations.

Example:

```
annotations = pd.read_csv('annotations.csv')
annotations.head()
```

Example Explanation:

- Loads annotations into a Pandas DataFrame.
- Displays the first few rows to verify data integrity.

2. Create DataBlock for Detection

What is Creating a DataBlock for Detection?

Defines the data processing pipeline for object detection.

Syntax:

```
def get_y(o):
    return annotations[annotations['image'] == o.name]
dblock = DataBlock(
    blocks=(ImageBlock, BBoxBlock, BBoxLblBlock),
    get_items=get_image_files,
    get_y=get_y,
    splitter=RandomSplitter(valid_pct=0.2),
    item_tfms=Resize(256),
    batch_tfms=aug_transforms()
)
```

Detailed Explanation:

- **Purpose:** Maps images to bounding boxes and labels.
- **Parameters:**
    - `ImageBlock`: Handles image inputs.
    - `BBoxBlock`: Processes bounding box coordinates.
    - `BBoxLblBlock`: Processes class labels for bounding boxes.
    - `get_y`: Function to retrieve bounding box annotations.
    - `splitter`: Splits data into training and validation sets.
- **Output:** DataBlock blueprint for object detection.

Example:

```
path = Path('images')
dblock = DataBlock(
    blocks=(ImageBlock, BBoxBlock, BBoxLblBlock),
    get_items=get_image_files,
    get_y=get_y,
    splitter=RandomSplitter(valid_pct=0.2)
)
```

Example Explanation:

- Links images with their corresponding bounding box annotations.
- Reserves 20% of the data for validation.

3. Apply Transformations
What are Transformations?
Preprocesses images and applies augmentations tailored for object detection.

Syntax:

```
dblock = dblock.new(item_tfms=Resize(256),
batch_tfms=aug_transforms())
```

Detailed Explanation:

- **Purpose:** Ensures uniform input size and introduces variations to improve model generalization.
- **Parameters:**
    - Resize: Rescales images and bounding boxes to a fixed size.
    - aug_transforms: Applies augmentations like flipping, rotation, or zoom.
- **Output:** Transformed and augmented images and annotations.

Example:

```
dls = dblock.dataloaders(path)
dls.show_batch(max_n=6, figsize=(8, 8))
```

Example Explanation:

- Visualizes a batch of transformed images with bounding boxes.
- Confirms proper alignment of transformations with annotations.

4. Train the Model

What is Training the Model?

Optimizes the object detection model to minimize loss and improve accuracy.

Syntax:

```
learn = cnn_learner(dls, resnet50, metrics=[accuracy])
learn.fine_tune(5)
```

Detailed Explanation:

- **Purpose:** Learns to predict bounding boxes and class labels.
- **Parameters:**
    - dls: Dataloaders containing transformed data.
    - resnet50: Pretrained ResNet-50 model for feature extraction.
    - metrics: List of metrics to evaluate model performance.
- **Output:** Trained model ready for evaluation.

Example:
```
learn = cnn_learner(dls, resnet50, metrics=[accuracy])
learn.fine_tune(3)
```
Example Explanation:
- Fine-tunes the ResNet-50 model for 3 epochs.
- Tracks accuracy and logs performance metrics.

5. Visualize Predictions
What is Visualizing Predictions?
Displays model predictions alongside ground truth annotations for analysis.
Syntax:
```
learn.show_results(max_n=6, figsize=(8, 8))
```
Detailed Explanation:
- **Purpose:** Evaluates the model's detection capabilities.
- **Parameters:**
  - max_n: Number of samples to display.
  - figsize: Size of the visualization.
- **Output:** Images with predicted bounding boxes and class labels.

Example:
```
learn.show_results(max_n=6, figsize=(10, 10))
```

Example Explanation:
- Visualizes six samples with predicted and actual bounding boxes.
- Highlights areas where the model excels or struggles.

Real-Life Project:

Project Name: Detecting Objects in Wildlife Images
Project Goal: Train a model to detect and classify animals in wildlife photographs.
Code for This Project:
```
from fastai.vision.all import *

# Load dataset
annotations = pd.read_csv('annotations.csv')
path = Path('images')
```

```python
def get_y(o):
    return annotations[annotations['image'] == o.name]
# Define DataBlock
dblock = DataBlock(
    blocks=(ImageBlock, BBoxBlock, BBoxLblBlock),
    get_items=get_image_files,
    get_y=get_y,
    splitter=RandomSplitter(valid_pct=0.2),
    item_tfms=Resize(256),
    batch_tfms=aug_transforms()
)
# Create Dataloaders
dls = dblock.dataloaders(path)

# Initialize Learner
learn = cnn_learner(dls, resnet50, metrics=[accuracy])

# Train the model
learn.fine_tune(5)

# Visualize results
learn.show_results(max_n=6, figsize=(10, 10))
```

Expected Output:
- Images with predicted bounding boxes and class labels.
- Improved detection accuracy over training epochs.
- Insights into model performance and areas for refinement.

Chapter - 8 Semantic Segmentation Using Fastai

Semantic segmentation assigns a label to every pixel in an image, enabling detailed understanding of scene composition. In this chapter, we explore how to implement semantic segmentation using the Fastai library, covering dataset preparation, model training, and performance evaluation.

Key Characteristics of Semantic Segmentation with Fastai:

- **Pixel-Level Classification:** Labels each pixel in an image with a class.
- **Pretrained Models:** Leverages architectures like UNet for efficient segmentation.
- **Data Augmentation:** Applies transformations specific to segmentation tasks.
- **Custom Loss Functions:** Supports weighted losses for imbalanced datasets.
- **Visualization Tools:** Displays predicted masks alongside ground truth for analysis.

Basic Steps for Semantic Segmentation:

1. **Prepare the Dataset:** Organize images and corresponding masks.
2. **Define the DataBlock:** Specify inputs, labels, and transformations.
3. **Initialize the Learner:** Use a segmentation-specific architecture.
4. **Train the Model:** Optimize using `fit` or `fine_tune` methods.
5. **Evaluate Results:** Visualize predictions and analyze performance.

Syntax Table:

SL No	Function	Syntax/Example	Description
1	Load Dataset	`untar_data(URLs.C AMVID)`	Downloads and extracts a dataset.
2	Define DataBlock for Segmentation	`DataBlock(blocks, get_items, splitter, ...)`	Defines the data pipeline for segmentation.
3	Apply Transformations	`Resize` and `aug_transforms()`	Preprocesses images and augments data.

4	Train the Model	`unet_learner(dls, resnet34, metrics)`	Initializes and trains a UNet model.
5	Visualize Predictions	`learn.show_result s()`	Displays predicted masks and ground truth.

Syntax Explanation:

1. Load Dataset

What is Loading a Dataset?

Fastai provides utilities to download and prepare datasets for segmentation tasks.

Syntax:

```
from fastai.vision.all import *
path = untar_data(URLs.CAMVID)
```

Detailed Explanation:

- **Purpose:** Prepares a dataset for segmentation tasks.
- **Parameters:**
    - `URLs.CAMVID`: A predefined URL for the CamVid dataset.
- **Output:** Path to the extracted dataset.

Example:

```
path = untar_data(URLs.CAMVID)
path.ls()
```

Example Explanation:

- Downloads the CamVid dataset and extracts it to the local file system.
- Lists the contents of the dataset directory for verification.

2. Define DataBlock for Segmentation

What is Creating a DataBlock for Segmentation?

The `DataBlock` API defines how images and masks are loaded, split, and processed.

Syntax:

```python
def label_func(fn):
    return path/'labels'/f'{fn.stem}_P{fn.suffix}'
dblock = DataBlock(
    blocks=(ImageBlock, MaskBlock(codes)),
    get_items=get_image_files,
    get_y=label_func,
    splitter=RandomSplitter(valid_pct=0.2),
    item_tfms=Resize(224),
    batch_tfms=aug_transforms()
)
```

Detailed Explanation:

- **Purpose:** Prepares the dataset pipeline for semantic segmentation.
- **Parameters:**
    - `ImageBlock`: Processes input images.
    - `MaskBlock`: Processes pixel-wise segmentation masks.
    - `get_items`: Retrieves file paths for images.
    - `get_y`: Retrieves corresponding masks.
    - `splitter`: Splits data into training and validation sets.
    - `item_tfms`: Applies transformations like resizing to individual items.
    - `batch_tfms`: Adds augmentations like flipping or rotation.
- **Output:** A blueprint for creating Dataloaders.

Example:

```python
def label_func(fn):
    return path/'labels'/f'{fn.stem}_P{fn.suffix}'
dblock = DataBlock(
    blocks=(ImageBlock, MaskBlock(codes)),
    get_items=get_image_files,
    get_y=label_func,
    splitter=RandomSplitter(valid_pct=0.2)
)
```

Example Explanation:

- Links images with their corresponding segmentation masks.

- Reserves 20% of the data for validation.

3. Apply Transformations
What are Transformations?
Preprocesses images and masks, applying augmentations for generalization.
Syntax:
```
dblock = dblock.new(item_tfms=Resize(224),
batch_tfms=aug_transforms())
```
Detailed Explanation:
- **Purpose:** Ensures uniform input size and introduces variations for better generalization.
- **Parameters:**
    - `Resize`: Rescales images and masks to a fixed size.
    - `aug_transforms`: Adds augmentations like flipping, rotation, or zoom.
- **Output:** Transformed and augmented images and masks.

Example:
```
dls = dblock.dataloaders(path/'images')
dls.show_batch(max_n=6, figsize=(8, 8))
```

Example Explanation:
- Visualizes a batch of transformed images with corresponding masks.
- Ensures proper alignment of augmentations with segmentation masks.

4. Train the Model
What is Training the Model?
Optimizes a segmentation model to minimize loss and improve accuracy.
Syntax:
```
learn = unet_learner(dls, resnet34, metrics=Dice())
learn.fine_tune(5)
```
Detailed Explanation:
- **Purpose:** Learns pixel-wise classifications for segmentation tasks.

- **Parameters:**
  - o `dls`: Dataloaders containing images and masks.
  - o `resnet34`: Pretrained ResNet-34 backbone for feature extraction.
  - o `metrics`: Evaluation metric like Dice coefficient.
- **Output:** Trained model ready for evaluation.

Example:
```
learn = unet_learner(dls, resnet34, metrics=Dice())
learn.fine_tune(3)
```

Example Explanation:
- Fine-tunes a UNet model with ResNet-34 backbone for 3 epochs.
- Tracks Dice coefficient to evaluate segmentation performance.

5. Visualize Predictions
What is Visualizing Predictions?
Displays model predictions alongside ground truth masks for analysis.
Syntax:
```
learn.show_results(max_n=6, figsize=(8, 8))
```
Detailed Explanation:
- **Purpose:** Evaluates the model's segmentation accuracy visually.
- **Parameters:**
  - o `max_n`: Number of samples to display.
  - o `figsize`: Size of the visualization.
- **Output:** Images with predicted and actual masks.

Example:
```
learn.show_results(max_n=6, figsize=(10, 10))
```

Example Explanation:
- Visualizes six samples with predicted and ground truth masks.
- Highlights areas where the model performs well or struggles.

Real-Life Project:
Project Name: Segmenting Road Scenes
Project Goal: Train a model to segment different elements in road scenes, such as roads, vehicles, and pedestrians.

Code for This Project:

```python
from fastai.vision.all import *

# Load dataset
path = untar_data(URLs.CAMVID)
codes = np.loadtxt(path/'codes.txt', dtype=str)
def label_func(fn):
    return path/'labels'/f'{fn.stem}_P{fn.suffix}'
# Define DataBlock
dblock = DataBlock(
    blocks=(ImageBlock, MaskBlock(codes)),
    get_items=get_image_files,
    get_y=label_func,
    splitter=RandomSplitter(valid_pct=0.2),
    item_tfms=Resize(224),
    batch_tfms=aug_transforms()
)
# Create Dataloaders
dls = dblock.dataloaders(path/'images')

# Initialize Learner
learn = unet_learner(dls, resnet34, metrics=Dice())

# Train the model
learn.fine_tune(5)

# Visualize results
learn.show_results(max_n=6, figsize=(10, 10))
```

Expected Output:
- Segmented images with predicted and ground truth masks.
- Improved segmentation accuracy over training epochs.
- Insights into model performance and areas for refinement.

Chapter - 9 Transfer Learning for Vision Tasks

Transfer learning leverages pretrained models to accelerate training and improve performance on vision tasks, especially when working with limited data. In this chapter, we explore the principles of transfer learning, its implementation in Fastai, and strategies for effective adaptation to new datasets.

Key Characteristics of Transfer Learning:

- **Pretrained Models:** Utilizes models trained on large datasets like ImageNet.
- **Fine-Tuning:** Adapts the pretrained model to the target task by training some or all layers.
- **Feature Transfer:** Reuses learned features from the pretrained model.
- **Faster Convergence:** Reduces training time by leveraging existing knowledge.
- **Improved Performance:** Often achieves higher accuracy on small datasets.

Basic Steps for Transfer Learning:

1. **Choose a Pretrained Model:** Select a model architecture suitable for the target task.
2. **Freeze Base Layers:** Start by training only the classification head.
3. **Unfreeze for Fine-Tuning:** Allow updates to the base layers to improve task-specific learning.
4. **Apply Data Augmentation:** Enhance model generalization.
5. **Evaluate and Interpret Results:** Analyze metrics and fine-tuning effectiveness.

Syntax Table:

SL No	Function	Syntax/Example	Description
1	Initialize Pretrained Model	`cnn_learner(dls, resnet34, metrics=accuracy)`	Sets up a pretrained model for transfer learning.
2	Fine-Tune Model	`learn.fine_tune(n_epochs)`	Fine-tunes the pretrained model for

			target task.
3	Freeze/Unfr eeze Layers	`learn.freeze()/` `learn.unfreeze()`	Freezes or unfreezes model layers.
4	Set Learning Rate	`learn.lr_find()`	Suggests optimal learning rates.
5	Interpret Results	`ClassificationInte rpretation.from_le arner()`	Provides tools for analyzing predictions.

Syntax Explanation:

1. Initialize Pretrained Model

What is Initializing a Pretrained Model?
Uses a model pretrained on a large dataset as a starting point for a new task.

Syntax:
```
from fastai.vision.all import *
learn = cnn_learner(dls, resnet34, metrics=accuracy)
```
Detailed Explanation:
- **Purpose:** Loads a pretrained model (e.g., ResNet-34) and prepares it for transfer learning.
- **Parameters:**
  - `dls`: Dataloaders containing training and validation data.
  - `resnet34`: Pretrained ResNet-34 architecture.
  - `metrics`: Metrics like `accuracy` for evaluation.
- **Output:** A configured Learner object ready for fine-tuning.

Example:
```
learn = cnn_learner(dls, resnet34, metrics=accuracy)
```
Example Explanation:
- Initializes a ResNet-34 model pretrained on ImageNet.
- Tracks accuracy during training and validation.

2. Fine-Tune Model

What is Fine-Tuning a Model?
Adapts the pretrained model to the target dataset by training both the classification head and the base layers.

Syntax:

```
learn.fine_tune(n_epochs)
```

Detailed Explanation:

- **Purpose:** Updates model weights to align with the new task.
- **Parameters:**
    - n_epochs: Number of epochs for fine-tuning.
- **How it Works:**
    - Initially trains only the classification head.
    - Gradually unfreezes and fine-tunes the base layers.
- **Output:** Trained model with improved performance on the target dataset.

Example:

```
learn.fine_tune(5)
```

Example Explanation:

- Fine-tunes the model for 5 epochs.
- Balances the use of pretrained knowledge with task-specific learning.

3. Freeze/Unfreeze Layers

What is Freezing and Unfreezing Layers?

Controls which layers of the model are trainable.

Syntax:

```
learn.freeze()
learn.unfreeze()
```

Detailed Explanation:

- **Purpose:**
    - freeze: Prevents updates to base layers, training only the head.
    - unfreeze: Allows updates to all layers for fine-tuning.
- **Use Case:**
    - Freezing layers retains pretrained features.
    - Unfreezing layers adapts the entire model to the new task.

Example:

```
learn.freeze()
```

```
learn.fit_one_cycle(3)
learn.unfreeze()
learn.fit_one_cycle(3)
```

Example Explanation:

- Trains the classification head for 3 epochs.
- Fine-tunes the entire model for another 3 epochs.

4. Set Learning Rate

What is Setting the Learning Rate?

Uses Fastai's learning rate finder to suggest optimal values for training.

Syntax:

```
learn.lr_find()
```

Detailed Explanation:

- **Purpose:** Identifies the learning rate that minimizes loss while maintaining stability.
- **Output:** Suggests a range of learning rates for fine-tuning.

Example:

```
learn.lr_find()
```

Example Explanation:

- Plots loss vs. learning rate.
- Helps choose an optimal value for fine-tuning.

5. Interpret Results

What is Interpreting Results?

Analyzes predictions to evaluate model performance and identify errors.

Syntax:

```
from fastai.vision.all import
ClassificationInterpretatio
interp =
ClassificationInterpretation.from_learner(learn)
interp.plot_confusion_matrix()
interp.plot_top_losses(5, nrows=1)
```

Detailed Explanation:

- **Purpose:** Evaluates the model's predictions against ground truth labels.
- **Key Methods:**
    - plot_confusion_matrix: Visualizes true vs. predicted
```
```

labels.
- o plot_top_losses: Highlights samples with the largest errors.
- **Output:** Graphical summaries for debugging and performance analysis.

Example:
```
interp =
ClassificationInterpretation.from_learner(learn)
interp.plot_confusion_matrix()
interp.plot_top_losses(3, nrows=1)
```
Example Explanation:
- Confusion matrix reveals misclassified categories.
- Top loss examples indicate areas for improvement.

Real-Life Project:

Project Name: Transfer Learning for Dog Breed Classification
Project Goal: Train a model to classify dog breeds using transfer learning with a ResNet backbone.
Code for This Project:
```
from fastai.vision.all import *
# Load dataset
path = untar_data(URLs.PETS) / 'images'
# Define DataBlock
dblock = DataBlock(
    blocks=(ImageBlock, CategoryBlock),
    get_items=get_image_files,
    get_y=parent_label,
    splitter=RandomSplitter(valid_pct=0.2),
    item_tfms=Resize(224),
    batch_tfms=aug_transforms()
)
# Create Dataloaders
dls = dblock.dataloaders(path)

# Initialize Learner
learn = cnn_learner(dls, resnet34, metrics=accuracy)
```

```
# Fine-tune the model
learn.fine_tune(5)

# Interpret results
interp =
ClassificationInterpretation.from_learner(learn)
interp.plot_confusion_matrix()
interp.plot_top_losses(5, nrows=1)
```
Expected Output:
- Improved classification accuracy over training epochs.
- Visualization of predictions and error analysis.
- Trained model ready for deployment.

Chapter - 10 Fine-Tuning Pretrained Vision Models

Fine-tuning pretrained vision models involves adapting a model trained on a large dataset (e.g., ImageNet) to a specific target task. This chapter covers strategies and techniques for fine-tuning using Fastai, including freezing layers, selecting optimal learning rates, and evaluating performance.

Key Characteristics of Fine-Tuning:

- **Knowledge Transfer:** Leverages feature representations learned from large datasets.
- **Layer Freezing:** Trains only specific parts of the model initially.
- **Learning Rate Optimization:** Employs learning rate schedules for efficient training.
- **Task-Specific Adaptation:** Adjusts weights for the target dataset.
- **Performance Boost:** Reduces training time and improves accuracy on small datasets.

Basic Steps for Fine-Tuning:

1. **Load a Pretrained Model:** Use a model trained on a large dataset as the starting point.
2. **Freeze Base Layers:** Train only the classification head initially.
3. **Set Learning Rates:** Use learning rate finder to identify optimal rates.
4. **Unfreeze and Fine-Tune:** Update all layers for task-specific learning.
5. **Evaluate and Interpret:** Assess the model's performance using metrics and visualization tools.

Syntax Table:

SL No	Function	Syntax/Example	Description
1	Initialize Pretrained Model	`cnn_learner(dls, resnet34, metrics=accuracy)`	Sets up a pretrained model for fine-tuning.
2	Freeze Layers	`learn.freeze()`	Freezes base layers to train only the head.
3	Find Learning Rate	`learn.lr_find()`	Suggests optimal learning rates.
4	Unfreeze Layers	`learn.unfreeze()`	Allows all layers to be updated.
5	Train with Discriminative LR	`learn.fit_one_cycle(n_epochs, lr)`	Fine-tunes with different learning rates.

Syntax Explanation:

1. Initialize Pretrained Model

What is Initializing a Pretrained Model?

Uses a pretrained model as the starting point for fine-tuning.

Syntax:

```
from fastai.vision.all import *
learn = cnn_learner(dls, resnet34, metrics=accuracy)
```

Detailed Explanation:

- **Purpose:** Loads a pretrained model and prepares it for transfer learning.
- **Parameters:**
  - o dls: Dataloaders containing training and validation data.
  - o resnet34: Pretrained ResNet-34 architecture.
  - o metrics: Evaluation metric like accuracy.
- **Output:** A configured Learner object ready for training.

Example:

```
learn = cnn_learner(dls, resnet34, metrics=accuracy)
```

Example Explanation:

- Initializes a ResNet-34 model pretrained on ImageNet.
- Tracks accuracy during training and validation.

2. Freeze Layers

What is Freezing Layers?
Prevents updates to base layers, allowing only the classification head to train.
Syntax:
```
learn.freeze()
```
Detailed Explanation:
- **Purpose:** Retains pretrained features in the base layers.
- **Output:** Trains only the classification head, reducing overfitting on small datasets.

Example:
```
learn.freeze()
learn.fit_one_cycle(3)
```
Example Explanation:
- Trains the classification head for 3 epochs.
- Keeps the pretrained base layers unchanged.

3. Find Learning Rate

What is Finding the Learning Rate?
Identifies an optimal learning rate for training.
Syntax:
```
learn.lr_find()
```
Detailed Explanation:
- **Purpose:** Plots loss vs. learning rate to suggest suitable values.
- **Output:** Learning rate range for efficient training.

Example:
```
learn.lr_find()
```
Example Explanation:
- Plots a graph showing how loss changes with learning rate.
- Helps select a learning rate that minimizes loss while maintaining stability.

4. Unfreeze Layers
What is Unfreezing Layers?
Allows updates to all layers for task-specific fine-tuning.
Syntax:
```
learn.unfreeze()
```
Detailed Explanation:
- **Purpose:** Enables the model to adapt pretrained features for the target task.
- **Output:** Updates all layers during training.

Example:
```
learn.unfreeze()
learn.fit_one_cycle(3, lr_max=slice(1e-5, 1e-3))
```

Example Explanation:
- Unfreezes all layers and fine-tunes with discriminative learning rates.
- Applies a lower learning rate to base layers and a higher rate to the head.

5. Train with Discriminative LR
What is Training with Discriminative Learning Rates?
Uses different learning rates for different parts of the model.
Syntax:
```
learn.fit_one_cycle(n_epochs, lr_max=slice(lr_low,
lr_high))
```
Detailed Explanation:
- **Purpose:** Fine-tunes layers with learning rates appropriate to their role.
- **Parameters:**
  - lr_low: Learning rate for base layers.
  - lr_high: Learning rate for the classification head.
- **Output:** Efficient and precise training.

Example:
```
learn.fit_one_cycle(5, lr_max=slice(1e-6, 1e-4))
```
Example Explanation:
- Trains for 5 epochs with lower learning rates for base layers and higher rates for the head.

- Balances fine-tuning with stability.

Real-Life Project:

Project Name: Fine-Tuning for Flower Classification

Project Goal: Train a model to classify flower species using a pretrained ResNet backbone.

Code for This Project:

```
from fastai.vision.all import *
# Load dataset
path = untar_data(URLs.FLOWERS)
# Define DataBlock
dblock = DataBlock(
    blocks=(ImageBlock, CategoryBlock),
    get_items=get_image_files,
    get_y=parent_label,
    splitter=RandomSplitter(valid_pct=0.2),
    item_tfms=Resize(224),
    batch_tfms=aug_transforms()
)
# Create Dataloaders
dls = dblock.dataloaders(path)
# Initialize Learner
learn = cnn_learner(dls, resnet34, metrics=accuracy)
# Freeze and Train Head
learn.freeze()
learn.fit_one_cycle(3)
# Unfreeze and Fine-Tune
learn.unfreeze()
learn.fit_one_cycle(5, lr_max=slice(1e-6, 1e-4))
# Evaluate Results
interp =
ClassificationInterpretation.from_learner(learn)
interp.plot_confusion_matrix()
interp.plot_top_losses(5, nrows=1)
```

Expected Output:

- Improved accuracy over training epochs.
- Visualization of misclassified samples and confusion matrix.
- Trained model ready for deployment.

Chapter – 11 Building and Using DataLoaders for Images

DataLoaders are essential in machine learning workflows, enabling efficient batching, shuffling, and preprocessing of datasets during training and validation. This chapter explains how to create, configure, and utilize DataLoaders in Fastai for image-based tasks.

Key Characteristics of DataLoaders:

- **Data Preparation:** Facilitates loading and preprocessing of datasets.
- **Batching:** Efficiently groups data into batches for training.
- **Shuffling:** Randomizes data order for robust training.
- **Transformations:** Applies augmentations and preprocessing to enhance generalization.
- **Integration:** Seamlessly integrates with the Fastai `Learner` object.

Basic Steps for Building DataLoaders:

1. **Prepare the Dataset:** Organize image files and labels into a structured format.
2. **Define a DataBlock:** Specify inputs, labels, and transformations.
3. **Create DataLoaders:** Convert the DataBlock into DataLoaders.
4. **Visualize Data:** Inspect batches to verify data integrity.
5. **Integrate with Learner:** Pass the DataLoaders to the `Learner` object for training.

Syntax Table:

SL No	Function	Syntax/Example	Description
1	Prepare Dataset	`untar_data(URLs.PETS )`	Downloads and extracts a dataset.
2	Define DataBlock	`DataBlock(blocks, get_items, splitter, ...)`	Creates a blueprint for DataLoaders.
3	Create DataLoad ers	`dblock.dataloaders(p ath)`	Converts a DataBlock into DataLoaders.
4	Show	`dls.show_batch(max_n`	Visualizes a batch of

	Batch	, figsize)	images and labels.
5	Pass to Learner	cnn_learner(dls, resnet34, metrics)	Integrates DataLoaders with the model.

Syntax Explanation:

1. Prepare Dataset

What is Preparing the Dataset?

Organizes and structures image datasets for use with DataLoaders.

Syntax:

```
from fastai.vision.all import *
path = untar_data(URLs.PETS)
```

Detailed Explanation:

- **Purpose:** Downloads and extracts datasets into a structured directory.
- **Parameters:**
  - URLs.PETS: URL for the Oxford-IIIT Pet Dataset.
- **Output:** Path to the extracted dataset.

Example:

```
path = untar_data(URLs.PETS) / 'images'
print(path.ls())
```

Example Explanation:

- Retrieves the path to the images directory.
- Verifies dataset structure by listing file contents.

2. Define DataBlock

What is Defining a DataBlock?

Specifies how images and labels are loaded, split, and processed.

Syntax:

```
dblock = DataBlock(
    blocks=(ImageBlock, CategoryBlock),
    get_items=get_image_files,
    get_y=parent_label,
    splitter=RandomSplitter(valid_pct=0.2),
    item_tfms=Resize(224),
    batch_tfms=aug_transforms()
)
```

Detailed Explanation:
- **Purpose:** Creates a blueprint for processing datasets.
- **Parameters:**
    - `blocks`: Specifies input-output types (e.g., images and categories).
    - `get_items`: Function to retrieve image files.
    - `get_y`: Function to extract labels from image paths.
    - `splitter`: Splits data into training and validation sets.
    - `item_tfms`: Resizes images to a uniform size.
    - `batch_tfms`: Applies augmentations like flipping or zooming.
- **Output:** A configurable DataBlock object.

Example:
```
dblock = DataBlock(
    blocks=(ImageBlock, CategoryBlock),
    get_items=get_image_files,
    get_y=parent_label,
    splitter=RandomSplitter(valid_pct=0.2)
)
```

Example Explanation:
- Defines a simple image classification pipeline.
- Reserves 20% of the data for validation.

3. Create DataLoaders

What are DataLoaders?
Handles data batching and preprocessing for training and validation.
Syntax:
```
dls = dblock.dataloaders(path)
```
Detailed Explanation:
- **Purpose:** Converts a DataBlock into training and validation DataLoaders.
- **Parameters:**
    - `path`: Path to the dataset directory.
- **Output:** A pair of DataLoaders (training and validation).

Example:

```
dls = dblock.dataloaders(path)
```

Example Explanation:

- Prepares DataLoaders for feeding data to the model.
- Handles batching, shuffling, and preprocessing automatically.

4. Show Batch

What is Showing a Batch?

Displays a batch of images and labels for inspection.

Syntax:

```
dls.show_batch(max_n=9, figsize=(6, 6))
```

Detailed Explanation:

- **Purpose:** Verifies the integrity and transformations of the dataset.
- **Parameters:**
  - max_n: Number of images to display.
  - figsize: Size of the visualization.
- **Output:** Grid of images with corresponding labels.

Example:

```
dls.show_batch(max_n=6, figsize=(8, 8))
```

Example Explanation:

- Displays six images and their labels.
- Confirms that the dataset is correctly loaded and processed.

5. Pass to Learner

What is Passing DataLoaders to Learner?

Integrates DataLoaders with a model for training and evaluation.

Syntax:

```
learn = cnn_learner(dls, resnet34, metrics=accuracy)
```

Detailed Explanation:

- **Purpose:** Prepares a model for training using the DataLoaders.
- **Parameters:**
  - dls: Training and validation DataLoaders.
  - resnet34: Pretrained ResNet-34 architecture.
  - metrics: Evaluation metric (e.g., accuracy).
- **Output:** Configured Learner object ready for training.

Example:

```
learn = cnn_learner(dls, resnet34, metrics=accuracy)
```

Example Explanation:

- Uses the prepared DataLoaders for model training.
- Tracks accuracy during training and validation.

Real-Life Project:

Project Name: Image Classification with DataLoaders

Project Goal: Build and train an image classifier using DataLoaders and a pretrained ResNet model.

Code for This Project:

```
from fastai.vision.all import *
# Load dataset
path = untar_data(URLs.PETS) / 'images'
# Define DataBlock
dblock = DataBlock(
    blocks=(ImageBlock, CategoryBlock),
    get_items=get_image_files,
    get_y=parent_label,
    splitter=RandomSplitter(valid_pct=0.2),
    item_tfms=Resize(224),
    batch_tfms=aug_transforms()
)
# Create DataLoaders
dls = dblock.dataloaders(path)
# Show a batch
dls.show_batch(max_n=6, figsize=(8, 8))
# Initialize Learner
learn = cnn_learner(dls, resnet34, metrics=accuracy)
# Train the model
learn.fine_tune(5)
# Evaluate Results
interp =
ClassificationInterpretation.from_learner(learn)
interp.plot_confusion_matrix()
interp.plot_top_losses(5, nrows=1)
```

Expected Output:

- Visualization of batches with images and labels.

Chapter - 12 Text Classification with Fastai

Text classification involves assigning labels to text data, enabling applications like sentiment analysis, spam detection, and topic classification. This chapter explores how to perform text classification using Fastai, covering dataset preparation, model training, and performance evaluation.

Key Characteristics of Text Classification with Fastai:

- **Pretrained Language Models:** Utilizes models like AWD-LSTM or Transformer architectures.
- **Text Preprocessing:** Handles tokenization, numericalization, and padding.
- **Transfer Learning:** Fine-tunes language models on the target dataset.
- **Metrics Tracking:** Evaluates performance using metrics like accuracy or F1-score.
- **Interpretation Tools:** Provides tools for analyzing and debugging predictions.

Basic Steps for Text Classification:

1. **Prepare the Dataset:** Organize text data and labels.
2. **Define a DataBlock:** Specify inputs, labels, and preprocessing steps.
3. **Create DataLoaders:** Convert the DataBlock into DataLoaders.
4. **Fine-Tune the Model:** Train the classifier using transfer learning.
5. **Evaluate Results:** Analyze model performance and interpret results.

Syntax Table:

SL No	Function	Syntax/Example	Description
1	Load Dataset	`untar_data(URLs.IMDB_SAMPLE)`	Downloads and extracts a text dataset.
2	Define DataBlock	`DataBlock(blocks, get_items, splitter, ...)`	Creates a blueprint for text classification.

3	Create DataLoaders	`dblock.dataloaders(path)`	Converts the DataBlock into DataLoaders.
4	Fine-Tune the Model	`text_classifier_learner(dls, AWD_LSTM, metrics)`	Initializes and trains a text classifier.
5	Interpret Results	`learn.show_results()`	Displays predictions and true labels.

Syntax Explanation:

1. Load Dataset

What is Loading a Dataset?

Downloads and prepares a dataset for text classification.

Syntax:

```
from fastai.text.all import *
path = untar_data(URLs.IMDB_SAMPLE)
```

Detailed Explanation:

- **Purpose:** Prepares text datasets for training by downloading and extracting the files.
- **Parameters:**
    - URLs.IMDB_SAMPLE: A predefined URL in Fastai pointing to a sample dataset of IMDB movie reviews.
- **Output:** Path to the extracted dataset directory containing text files or structured data.

Example:

```
path = untar_data(URLs.IMDB_SAMPLE)
print(path.ls())
```

Example Explanation:

- Downloads the IMDB sample dataset into a local directory.
- Lists the files and directories inside the extracted dataset to verify its structure.
- This step ensures that the dataset is correctly loaded and accessible.

2. Define DataBlock

What is Defining a DataBlock?
Specifies how text and labels are loaded, split, and processed for training.
Syntax:
```
dblock = DataBlock(
    blocks=(TextBlock.from_folder(), CategoryBlock),
    get_y=parent_label,
    splitter=RandomSplitter(valid_pct=0.2)
)
```
Detailed Explanation:
- **Purpose:** Sets up a flexible data pipeline for text classification.
- **Parameters:**
    - `TextBlock.from_folder()`: Configures the pipeline to process text data from folders, handling tokenization, numericalization, and padding.
    - `CategoryBlock`: Defines the target output as categorical labels.
    - `get_y`: Function to extract labels from folder names (e.g., pos and neg for positive and negative sentiment).
    - `splitter`: Splits the dataset into training and validation sets, with 20% reserved for validation in this case.
- **Output:** A `DataBlock` object ready to be converted into DataLoaders.

Example:
```
dblock = DataBlock(
    blocks=(TextBlock.from_folder(), CategoryBlock),
    get_y=parent_label,
    splitter=RandomSplitter(valid_pct=0.2)
)
```
Example Explanation:
- Prepares the dataset for training by reading text files from subfolders.
- Automatically assigns labels based on the parent folder names.
- Ensures the data is split into training and validation subsets for model evaluation.

3. Create DataLoaders

What are DataLoaders?
Handles tokenization, numericalization, batching, and padding of text data for model input.
Syntax:
```
dls = dblock.dataloaders(path)
```
Detailed Explanation:

- **Purpose:** Converts the `DataBlock` into `DataLoaders` for feeding data into the model during training and validation.
- **How it Works:**
    - Tokenizes text data into smaller units (words or subwords).
    - Converts tokens into numerical representations for model processing.
    - Handles batching and ensures consistent input lengths using padding.
- **Parameters:**
    - `path`: Directory containing the text files.
- **Output:** DataLoaders for training and validation.

Example:
```
dls = dblock.dataloaders(path)
dls.show_batch(max_n=6)
```
Example Explanation:

- Creates batches of tokenized text and their corresponding labels.
- Displays a batch of text samples along with their predicted or actual labels.
- Helps verify that text processing and batching are correctly implemented.

4. Fine-Tune the Model
What is Fine-Tuning the Model?
Adapts a pretrained language model to the target text classification task.
Syntax:
```
learn = text_classifier_learner(dls, AWD_LSTM,
metrics=accuracy)
```

```
learn.fine_tune(3)
```
Detailed Explanation:

- **Purpose:** Fine-tunes a pretrained language model to classify text based on the target dataset.
- **Parameters:**
  - `dls`: DataLoaders containing tokenized text and their corresponding labels.
  - AWD_LSTM: Pretrained AWD-LSTM language model for transfer learning.
  - `metrics`: Metrics such as `accuracy` to monitor training progress.
- **Output:** Trained text classification model.

Example:
```
learn = text_classifier_learner(dls, AWD_LSTM,
metrics=accuracy)
learn.fine_tune(5)
```
Example Explanation:

- Leverages the pretrained AWD-LSTM model to quickly adapt to the target dataset.
- Fine-tunes for 5 epochs, optimizing both the base model and the classification head.
- Tracks performance metrics such as accuracy after each epoch.

5. Interpret Results

What is Interpreting Results?

Analyzes predictions and provides insights into model performance.

Syntax:
```
learn.show_results(max_n=6)
```
Detailed Explanation:

- **Purpose:** Displays a visual summary of the model's predictions alongside ground truth labels.
- **How it Works:**
  - Highlights correctly classified samples and misclassifications.
  - Useful for debugging and identifying areas of improvement.
- **Parameters:**

o   max_n: Specifies the number of samples to display.
- **Output:** Grid of text samples with predicted and actual labels.

Example:
```
learn.show_results(max_n=6)
```
Example Explanation:
- Visualizes six text samples with their true labels and predicted labels.
- Helps evaluate the model's performance qualitatively and identify common errors.

Real-Life Project:

Project Name: Sentiment Analysis on IMDB Reviews

Project Goal: Train a model to classify movie reviews as positive or negative.

Code for This Project:
```
from fastai.text.all import *
# Load dataset
path = untar_data(URLs.IMDB_SAMPLE)
# Define DataBlock
dblock = DataBlock(
    blocks=(TextBlock.from_folder(), CategoryBlock),
    get_y=parent_label,
    splitter=RandomSplitter(valid_pct=0.2)
)
# Create DataLoaders
dls = dblock.dataloaders(path)
# Initialize Learner
learn = text_classifier_learner(dls, AWD_LSTM,
metrics=accuracy)
# Fine-Tune the Model
learn.fine_tune(5)
# Evaluate Results
learn.show_results(max_n=6)
```

Expected Output:
- Improved accuracy over training epochs.
- Visualization of predictions and misclassifications.
- Trained model ready for deployment.

Chapter - 13 Working with Language Models in Fastai

Language models are foundational tools in natural language processing (NLP), enabling tasks like text generation, sentiment analysis, and machine translation. This chapter explores how to build, fine-tune, and evaluate language models using Fastai.

Key Characteristics of Language Models in Fastai:

- **Pretrained Models:** Leverages models like AWD-LSTM or Transformers for faster and more accurate results.
- **Sequential Processing:** Handles text sequences efficiently using tokenization and numericalization.
- **Transfer Learning:** Fine-tunes pretrained models on specific datasets.
- **Text Generation:** Supports generating coherent text sequences.
- **Metrics Tracking:** Provides tools for evaluating perplexity and other metrics.

Basic Steps for Working with Language Models:

1. **Prepare the Dataset:** Organize text data for training.
2. **Define a DataBlock:** Specify inputs, preprocessing steps, and splitting strategy.
3. **Create DataLoaders:** Convert the DataBlock into DataLoaders.
4. **Train the Language Model:** Fine-tune a pretrained model for your dataset.
5. **Generate and Evaluate Text:** Use the model to create new text and evaluate its coherence.

Syntax Table:

SL No	Function	Syntax/Example	Description
1	Load Dataset	`untar_data(URLs.IMDB_SAMPLE)`	Downloads and extracts a text dataset.
2	Define DataBlock	`DataBlock(blocks, get_items, splitter, ...)`	Creates a blueprint for training language models.
3	Create DataLoader	`dblock.dataloaders(path)`	Converts the DataBlock into DataLoaders.

		s		
4	Train the Language Model	`language_model_lea rner(dls, AWD_LSTM, metrics)`	Initializes and trains a language model.	
5	Generate Text	`learn.predict()`	Generates text from a trained language model.	

Syntax Explanation:

1. Load Dataset

What is Loading a Dataset?

Organizes text data for training and validation.

Syntax:

```
from fastai.text.all import *
path = untar_data(URLs.IMDB_SAMPLE)
```

Detailed Explanation:

- **Purpose:** Prepares a text dataset for language modeling by downloading and extracting the files.
- **Parameters:**
    - `URLs.IMDB_SAMPLE`: A predefined URL for the IMDB sample dataset.
- **Output:** Path to the dataset directory containing text files or structured data.

Example:

```
path = untar_data(URLs.IMDB_SAMPLE)
print(path.ls())
```

Example Explanation:

- Downloads the IMDB sample dataset to the local machine.
- Lists the contents of the dataset directory for verification.

2. Define DataBlock

What is Defining a DataBlock?

Sets up a pipeline for loading, tokenizing, and splitting text data.

Syntax:

```
dblock = DataBlock(
    blocks=(TextBlock.from_folder(is_lm=True),),
    get_items=get_text_files,
```

```
    splitter=RandomSplitter(valid_pct=0.2)
)
```

Detailed Explanation:

- **Purpose:** Prepares text data for language modeling.
- **Parameters:**
  - `TextBlock.from_folder(is_lm=True)`: Configures the pipeline for language modeling by processing text as sequences.
  - `get_items`: Retrieves text files from the specified directory.
  - `splitter`: Splits the dataset into training and validation subsets.
- **Output:** A `DataBlock` object ready for conversion into DataLoaders.

Example:

```
dblock = DataBlock(
    blocks=(TextBlock.from_folder(is_lm=True),),
    get_items=get_text_files,
    splitter=RandomSplitter(valid_pct=0.2)
)
```

Example Explanation:

- Configures a pipeline for tokenizing text files into sequences.
- Ensures that 20% of the data is reserved for validation.

3. Create DataLoaders

What are DataLoaders?

Handles tokenization, numericalization, and batching of text sequences.

Syntax:

```
dls = dblock.dataloaders(path)
```

Detailed Explanation:

- **Purpose:** Converts the `DataBlock` into DataLoaders for training and validation.
- **How it Works:**
  - Tokenizes text data into smaller units (words or subwords).

- o Converts tokens into numerical representations for model input.
  - o Handles batching and ensures consistent sequence lengths.
- **Output:** DataLoaders for training and validation.

Example:
```
dls = dblock.dataloaders(path)
dls.show_batch(max_n=5)
```
Example Explanation:
- Displays a batch of tokenized text sequences.
- Ensures that the text data is properly processed and ready for model input.

4. Train the Language Model

What is Training the Language Model?

Fine-tunes a pretrained language model on the target dataset.

Syntax:
```
learn = language_model_learner(dls, AWD_LSTM,
metrics=Perplexity())
learn.fine_tune(3)
```
Detailed Explanation:
- **Purpose:** Adapts a pretrained language model to the dataset by fine-tuning it.
- **Parameters:**
  - o dls: DataLoaders containing tokenized text sequences.
  - o AWD_LSTM: Pretrained AWD-LSTM model for sequential data.
  - o metrics: Perplexity metric to evaluate the model's text generation capability.
- **Output:** A trained language model capable of generating coherent text.

Example:
```
learn = language_model_learner(dls, AWD_LSTM,
metrics=Perplexity())
learn.fine_tune(5)
```

Example Explanation:

- Fine-tunes the AWD-LSTM model for 5 epochs.
- Tracks the perplexity metric to monitor the quality of text predictions.

5. Generate Text

What is Generating Text?

Uses the trained language model to create new text sequences.

Syntax:

```
learn.predict("Once upon a time", n_words=20)
```

Detailed Explanation:

- **Purpose:** Generates a continuation of a given text prompt using the trained model.
- **Parameters:**
  - `"Once upon a time"`: Initial text prompt.
  - `n_words`: Number of words to generate.
- **Output:** A string of generated text extending the input prompt.

Example:

```
output = learn.predict("The future of AI", n_words=15)
print(output)
```

Example Explanation:

- Generates a text sequence based on the prompt "The future of AI".
- Helps evaluate the model's ability to produce coherent and contextually relevant text.

Real-Life Project:

Project Name: Text Generation with IMDB Reviews

Project Goal: Train a language model to generate movie review text based on existing IMDB reviews.

Code for This Project:

```
from fastai.text.all import *
# Load dataset
path = untar_data(URLs.IMDB_SAMPLE)
# Define DataBlock
dblock = DataBlock(
    blocks=(TextBlock.from_folder(is_lm=True),),
    get_items=get_text_files,
    splitter=RandomSplitter(valid_pct=0.2)
```

```python
# Create DataLoaders
dls = dblock.dataloaders(path)
# Initialize Learner
learn = language_model_learner(dls, AWD_LSTM,
metrics=Perplexity())
# Fine-Tune the Model
learn.fine_tune(5)
# Generate Text
output = learn.predict("The movie was", n_words=20)
print(output)
```

Expected Output:
- Improved perplexity over training epochs.
- Coherent and contextually relevant text generated by the model.
- Trained language model ready for text generation tasks.

Chapter - 14 Transfer Learning for NLP Tasks

Transfer learning for natural language processing (NLP) involves leveraging pretrained language models to improve the performance and efficiency of downstream tasks such as text classification, sentiment analysis, and question answering. This chapter explores how to implement transfer learning for NLP tasks using Fastai, covering dataset preparation, model fine-tuning, and performance evaluation.

Key Characteristics of Transfer Learning for NLP:

- **Pretrained Models:** Utilizes models like AWD-LSTM or Transformer-based architectures trained on large corpora.
- **Fine-Tuning:** Adapts pretrained models to specific datasets and tasks.
- **Layer Freezing:** Gradually unfreezes layers for optimal learning.
- **Efficiency:** Reduces training time and data requirements.
- **Improved Performance:** Leverages learned representations for better generalization.

Basic Steps for Transfer Learning in NLP:

1. **Prepare the Dataset:** Organize text data for training and validation.
2. **Define a DataBlock:** Specify text inputs, labels, and preprocessing steps.
3. **Create DataLoaders:** Convert the DataBlock into DataLoaders.
4. **Fine-Tune the Model:** Adapt a pretrained model to the target task.
5. **Evaluate and Interpret:** Assess model performance using metrics and interpret results.

Syntax Table:

SL No	Function	Syntax/Example	Description
1	Load Dataset	`untar_data(URLs.IMDB_SAMPLE)`	Downloads and extracts a text dataset.
2	Define DataBlock	`DataBlock(blocks, get_items, splitter, ...)`	Specifies preprocessing for NLP tasks.

3	Create DataLoad ers	`dblock.dataloaders( path)`	Converts the DataBlock into DataLoaders.
4	Fine-Tune the Model	`text_classifier_lea rner(dls, AWD_LSTM, metrics)`	Initializes and fine-tunes a pretrained model.
5	Evaluate and Interpret	`learn.show_results( )`	Displays predictions and evaluates performance.

Syntax Explanation:

1. Load Dataset
What is Loading a Dataset?
Organizes and prepares text data for training.
Syntax:
```
from fastai.text.all import *
path = untar_data(URLs.IMDB_SAMPLE)
```
Detailed Explanation:
- **Purpose:** Downloads and extracts a dataset for NLP tasks.
- **Parameters:**
  - URLs.IMDB_SAMPLE: A predefined URL pointing to the IMDB sample dataset.
- **Output:** Path to the extracted dataset directory containing text files.

Example:
```
path = untar_data(URLs.IMDB_SAMPLE)
print(path.ls())
```

Example Explanation:
- Downloads the IMDB sample dataset to a local directory.
- Lists the files within the extracted directory to verify dataset structure.

2. Define DataBlock
What is Defining a DataBlock?
Configures how text data is processed and split for training.
Syntax:

```
dblock = DataBlock(
    blocks=(TextBlock.from_folder(), CategoryBlock),
    get_y=parent_label,
    splitter=RandomSplitter(valid_pct=0.2)
)
```

Detailed Explanation:

- **Purpose:** Creates a pipeline for tokenizing, numericalizing, and splitting text data.
- **Parameters:**
    - `TextBlock.from_folder()`: Processes text data from folder structures.
    - `CategoryBlock`: Handles categorical labels for classification tasks.
    - `get_y`: Function to extract labels from folder names (e.g., pos and neg).
    - `splitter`: Splits data into training and validation sets.
- **Output:** A `DataBlock` object ready for creating DataLoaders.

Example:

```
dblock = DataBlock(
    blocks=(TextBlock.from_folder(), CategoryBlock),
    get_y=parent_label,
    splitter=RandomSplitter(valid_pct=0.2)
)
```

Example Explanation:

- Configures the text data pipeline for classification tasks.
- Ensures that 20% of the data is used for validation.

3. Create DataLoaders

What are DataLoaders?

Handles batching, tokenization, and numericalization of text data.

Syntax:

```
dls = dblock.dataloaders(path)
```

Detailed Explanation:

- **Purpose:** Converts the `DataBlock` into `DataLoaders` for model training and validation.
- **How it Works:**
    - Tokenizes text into words or subwords.
```
```

- o   Converts tokens into numerical representations.
- o   Handles batching and ensures consistent sequence lengths with padding.
- **Output:** DataLoaders ready for training.

Example:

```
dls = dblock.dataloaders(path)
dls.show_batch(max_n=5)
```

Example Explanation:

- Displays a batch of tokenized text samples with their labels.
- Verifies that preprocessing and batching are functioning as expected.

4. Fine-Tune the Model

What is Fine-Tuning the Model?

Adapts a pretrained model for the target NLP task.

Syntax:

```
learn = text_classifier_learner(dls, AWD_LSTM,
metrics=accuracy)
learn.fine_tune(3)
```

Detailed Explanation:

- **Purpose:** Fine-tunes a pretrained model to classify text data.
- **Parameters:**
  - o   `dls`: DataLoaders containing tokenized text and labels.
  - o   AWD_LSTM: Pretrained AWD-LSTM model for sequential data.
  - o   `metrics`: Metrics like `accuracy` to monitor performance.
- **Output:** A trained text classification model.

Example:

```
learn = text_classifier_learner(dls, AWD_LSTM,
metrics=accuracy)
learn.fine_tune(5)
```

Example Explanation:

- Fine-tunes the AWD-LSTM model for 5 epochs on the target dataset.
- Tracks accuracy during training and validation.

5. Evaluate and Interpret

What is Evaluating and Interpreting?

Analyzes model predictions and evaluates its performance.

Syntax:

```
learn.show_results(max_n=6)
```

Detailed Explanation:

- **Purpose:** Displays predicted labels alongside true labels for analysis.
- **Parameters:**
    - max_n: Number of samples to display.
- **Output:** Visualization of predictions and true labels.

Example:

```
learn.show_results(max_n=6)
```

Example Explanation:

- Displays six text samples with their actual and predicted labels.
- Highlights areas where the model performs well or struggles.

Real-Life Project:

Project Name: Sentiment Analysis with Transfer Learning

Project Goal: Use a pretrained language model to classify IMDB reviews as positive or negative.

Code for This Project:

```
from fastai.text.all import *
# Load dataset
path = untar_data(URLs.IMDB_SAMPLE)
# Define DataBlock
dblock = DataBlock(
    blocks=(TextBlock.from_folder(), CategoryBlock),
    get_y=parent_label,
    splitter=RandomSplitter(valid_pct=0.2)
)
# Create DataLoaders
dls = dblock.dataloaders(path)
# Initialize Learner
learn = text_classifier_learner(dls, AWD_LSTM,
metrics=accuracy)
```

```
# Fine-Tune the Model
learn.fine_tune(5)
# Evaluate Results
learn.show_results(max_n=6)
```

Expected Output:

- Improved accuracy over training epochs.
- Visualization of predictions and misclassifications.
- Trained model ready for deployment.

Chapter - 15 Tokenization and Preprocessing Text Data

Tokenization and preprocessing are foundational steps in natural language processing (NLP), converting raw text into a structured format that can be processed by machine learning models. This chapter explores how Fastai simplifies these processes, covering techniques for tokenization, numericalization, padding, and cleaning text data.

Key Characteristics of Tokenization and Preprocessing in Fastai:

- **Tokenization:** Splits raw text into smaller units such as words or subwords.
- **Numericalization:** Converts tokens into numerical indices for model input.
- **Text Cleaning:** Removes unnecessary elements like stopwords, punctuation, and special characters.
- **Batch Processing:** Ensures consistent sequence lengths through padding or truncation.
- **Integration with Pipelines:** Seamlessly integrates preprocessing into Fastai's DataBlock and DataLoader pipelines.

Basic Steps for Tokenization and Preprocessing:

1. **Load Raw Text Data:** Organize and inspect text data for preprocessing.
2. **Tokenize Text:** Split raw text into smaller tokens.
3. **Numericalize Tokens:** Map tokens to numerical indices.
4. **Clean Text Data:** Remove unwanted elements to improve model performance.
5. **Prepare for Batching:** Ensure uniform sequence lengths with padding or truncation.

Syntax Table:

SL No	Function	Syntax/Example	Description
1	Load Dataset	`untar_data(URLs.IMDB_SAMPLE)`	Downloads and extracts a text dataset.
2	Tokenize Text	`tokenizer = Tokenizer()`	Splits text into tokens.
3	Numericalize	`numericalizer =`	Converts tokens to

	Tokens	Numericalize()	numerical indices.
4	Clean Text	clean_text(text)	Removes stopwords, punctuation, and noise.
5	Pad/Truncate Sequences	pad_sequence(sequences, maxlen)	Ensures consistent input length.

Syntax Explanation:

1. Load Dataset

What is Loading a Dataset?

Organizes raw text data for preprocessing.

Syntax:

```
from fastai.text.all import *
path = untar_data(URLs.IMDB_SAMPLE)
```

Detailed Explanation:

- **Purpose:** Downloads and extracts a dataset for preprocessing.
- **Parameters:**
    - URLs.IMDB_SAMPLE: A predefined URL pointing to the IMDB sample dataset.
- **Output:** Path to the extracted dataset directory containing raw text files.

Example:

```
path = untar_data(URLs.IMDB_SAMPLE)
print(path.ls())
```

Example Explanation:

- Downloads the IMDB sample dataset to a local directory.
- Lists the contents of the extracted directory to verify dataset structure.

2. Tokenize Text

What is Tokenizing Text?

Breaks raw text into smaller units for easier processing.

Syntax:

```
tokenizer = Tokenizer()
tokens = tokenizer("This is a sample text.")
```

Detailed Explanation:

- **Purpose:** Splits sentences into words, subwords, or other meaningful units.

- **Parameters:**
  - ○ Tokenizer(): A Fastai utility for tokenizing text.
  - ○ Input text: The raw string to be tokenized.
- **Output:** A list of tokens representing the input text.

Example:

```
tokenizer = Tokenizer()
tokens = tokenizer("Fastai simplifies text
processing.")
print(tokens)
```

Example Explanation:

- Tokenizes the sentence into words such as ['fastai', 'simplifies', 'text', 'processing'].
- Helps prepare text for numericalization.

3. Numericalize Tokens

What is Numericalizing Tokens?

Maps tokens to numerical indices for model input.

Syntax:

```
numericalizer = Numericalize()
numerical_indices = numericalizer(tokens)
```

Detailed Explanation:

- **Purpose:** Converts string tokens into integers that models can process.
- **Parameters:**
  - ○ Numericalize(): A Fastai class that maps tokens to unique indices.
  - ○ tokens: List of tokens to be numericalized.
- **Output:** A list of integers corresponding to the input tokens.

Example:

```
numericalizer = Numericalize()
numerical_indices = numericalizer(['fastai',
'simplifies', 'text', 'processing'])
print(numerical_indices)
```

Example Explanation:

- Maps each token to a unique integer, e.g., [12, 45, 67, 89].
- Enables models to process text as numerical data.

4. Clean Text
What is Cleaning Text?
Removes noise such as stopwords, punctuation, and special characters.
Syntax:
```
def clean_text(text):
    text = re.sub(r'[^\w\s]', '', text)   # Remove
punctuation
    text = text.lower()                    # Convert to
lowercase
    return text
```
Detailed Explanation:
- **Purpose:** Prepares raw text for analysis by removing unnecessary elements.
- **Parameters:**
  - text: The raw string to be cleaned.
- **Output:** A cleaned string ready for tokenization.

Example:
```
cleaned_text = clean_text("Fastai simplifies, text
processing!")
print(cleaned_text)
```
Example Explanation:

- Converts the input to lowercase and removes punctuation, resulting in `fastai simplifies text processing`.

5. Pad/Truncate Sequences
What is Padding or Truncating Sequences?
Ensures uniform sequence lengths by adding padding or truncating.
Syntax:
```
from torch.nn.utils.rnn import pad_sequence
padded_sequences = pad_sequence(sequences,
batch_first=True, padding_value=0)
```
Detailed Explanation:
- **Purpose:** Aligns sequences to the same length for batch processing.
- **Parameters:**
  - sequences: List of numericalized token sequences.
  - padding_value: Integer value used for padding shorter

sequences.
- **Output:** A tensor of padded sequences.

Example:
```
import torch
sequences = [torch.tensor([1, 2, 3]), torch.tensor([4,
5])]
padded_sequences = pad_sequence(sequences,
batch_first=True, padding_value=0)
print(padded_sequences)
```
Example Explanation:
- Pads shorter sequences with zeros, resulting in a uniform shape like: [[1, 2, 3],
   [4, 5, 0]]
- Ensures compatibility with batch processing.

Real-Life Project:
Project Name: Preprocessing for Sentiment Analysis
Project Goal: Clean, tokenize, and numericalize text data for training a sentiment analysis model.
Code for This Project:
```
from fastai.text.all import *
# Load dataset
path = untar_data(URLs.IMDB_SAMPLE)
# Define DataBlock
dblock = DataBlock(
    blocks=(TextBlock.from_folder(), CategoryBlock),
    get_y=parent_label,
    splitter=RandomSplitter(valid_pct=0.2)
)
# Create DataLoaders
dls = dblock.dataloaders(path)
# Inspect a Batch
dls.show_batch(max_n=5)
```
Expected Output:
- Tokenized and numericalized text batches.
- Consistent sequence lengths with padding.
- Text data ready for model input.

Chapter - 16 Sentiment Analysis with Fastai's Text Modules

Sentiment analysis classifies text data into categories such as positive, negative, or neutral sentiment. Using Fastai's text modules, we can efficiently build, fine-tune, and evaluate sentiment analysis models. This chapter guides you through preparing datasets, training models, and interpreting results for sentiment analysis tasks.

Key Characteristics of Sentiment Analysis with Fastai:

- **Pretrained Language Models:** Utilizes pretrained models like AWD-LSTM for efficient training.
- **Transfer Learning:** Fine-tunes language models for specific sentiment analysis tasks.
- **Integrated Preprocessing:** Handles tokenization, numericalization, and text cleaning.
- **Metrics Tracking:** Monitors metrics like accuracy during training.
- **Interpretation Tools:** Provides insights into model performance and error analysis.

Basic Steps for Sentiment Analysis:

1. **Prepare the Dataset:** Organize text data and labels.
2. **Define a DataBlock:** Specify inputs, labels, and preprocessing steps.
3. **Create DataLoaders:** Convert the DataBlock into DataLoaders.
4. **Fine-Tune the Model:** Train a pretrained model on the sentiment analysis dataset.
5. **Evaluate and Interpret:** Analyze model predictions and performance.

Syntax Table:

SL No	Function	Syntax/Example	Description
1	Load Dataset	`untar_data(URLs.IMDB_SAMPLE)`	Downloads and extracts a text dataset.
2	Define DataBlock	`DataBlock(blocks, get_items, splitter, ...)`	Specifies data processing for text classification.

3	Create DataLoaders	`dblock.dataloaders(path)`	Converts the DataBlock into DataLoaders.
4	Train the Model	`text_classifier_learner(dls, AWD_LSTM, metrics)`	Initializes and trains a sentiment analysis model.
5	Evaluate and Interpret	`learn.show_results()`	Displays predictions and evaluates performance.

Syntax Explanation:

1. Load Dataset

What is Loading a Dataset?

Organizes and prepares text data for sentiment analysis.

Syntax:

```
from fastai.text.all import *
path = untar_data(URLs.IMDB_SAMPLE)
```

Detailed Explanation:

- **Purpose:** Downloads and extracts a text dataset for sentiment analysis.
- **Parameters:**
  - `URLs.IMDB_SAMPLE`: A predefined URL pointing to a sample IMDB dataset.
- **Output:** Path to the extracted dataset directory containing text files.

Example:

```
path = untar_data(URLs.IMDB_SAMPLE)
print(path.ls())
```

Example Explanation:

- Downloads the IMDB sample dataset to a local directory.
- Lists the files in the dataset directory to verify its structure.
- Verifies that the data is organized and ready for further processing.

2. Define DataBlock

What is Defining a DataBlock?

Specifies how text data and labels are loaded, processed, and split.

Syntax:

```
dblock = DataBlock(
    blocks=(TextBlock.from_folder(), CategoryBlock),
    get_y=parent_label,
    splitter=RandomSplitter(valid_pct=0.2)
)
```

Detailed Explanation:

- **Purpose:** Configures the pipeline for tokenizing, numericalizing, and splitting text data.
- **Parameters:**
  - `TextBlock.from_folder()`: Processes text data from folder structures, automatically handling tokenization and numericalization.
  - `CategoryBlock`: Defines the target variable as categorical labels for classification tasks (e.g., `positive` or `negative`).
  - `get_y`: Extracts the label from the folder names containing the text data.
  - `splitter`: Splits the dataset into training and validation subsets, with 20% reserved for validation.
- **Output:** A `DataBlock` object that outlines how to process the dataset.

Example:

```
dblock = DataBlock(
    blocks=(TextBlock.from_folder(), CategoryBlock),
    get_y=parent_label,
    splitter=RandomSplitter(valid_pct=0.2)
)
```

Example Explanation:

- Defines the structure of the data processing pipeline for sentiment analysis.
- Ensures a proper split between training and validation data for model evaluation.
- Prepares the dataset for efficient model input.

3. Create DataLoaders
What are DataLoaders?
Prepares text data for training by handling tokenization, numericalization, and batching.
Syntax:
```
dls = dblock.dataloaders(path)
```

Detailed Explanation:
- **Purpose:** Converts the `DataBlock` into `DataLoaders` for feeding data into the model during training and validation.
- **How it Works:**
    ○ Text is tokenized into smaller units (e.g., words or subwords).
    ○ Tokens are converted into numerical indices that represent unique words.
    ○ Data is grouped into batches of consistent sequence lengths using padding for efficiency.
- **Output:** Training and validation DataLoaders.

Example:
```
dls = dblock.dataloaders(path)
dls.show_batch(max_n=5)
```
Example Explanation:
- Displays a batch of processed text samples and their corresponding sentiment labels.
- Allows verification that tokenization, numericalization, and batching are working as expected.
- Ensures the dataset is ready for model training.

4. Train the Model
What is Training the Model?
Fine-tunes a pretrained language model for sentiment classification.
Syntax:
```
learn = text_classifier_learner(dls, AWD_LSTM,
metrics=accuracy)
learn.fine_tune(3)
```
Detailed Explanation:
- **Purpose:** Leverages a pretrained model (e.g., AWD-LSTM) to

efficiently classify sentiment in text data.

- **Parameters:**
  - o `dls`: DataLoaders containing tokenized and numericalized text with labels.
  - o `AWD_LSTM`: A pretrained language model optimized for sequential text data.
  - o `metrics`: Metric(s) to monitor during training, such as `accuracy`.
- **Process:**
  - o Initially freezes the base layers of the model to train only the classifier head.
  - o Gradually unfreezes the base layers for fine-tuning, adapting the model to the dataset.
- **Output:** A fine-tuned sentiment analysis model.

Example:
```
learn = text_classifier_learner(dls, AWD_LSTM,
metrics=accuracy)
learn.fine_tune(5)
```
Example Explanation:
- Initializes a learner object with the AWD-LSTM model and DataLoaders.
- Fine-tunes the model for 5 epochs, adapting pretrained representations to the sentiment dataset.
- Monitors accuracy to ensure the model improves with training.

5. Evaluate and Interpret
What is Evaluating and Interpreting?
Analyzes model predictions and evaluates its performance.
Syntax:
```
learn.show_results(max_n=6)
```
Detailed Explanation:
- **Purpose:** Displays the model's predictions alongside the true labels for analysis.
- **Parameters:**
  - o `max_n`: Specifies the number of samples to display.
- **Output:** A tabular or visual comparison of predicted and actual labels.

Example:
```
learn.show_results(max_n=6)
```
Example Explanation:
- Shows six examples of text data, their actual sentiment labels, and the model's predictions.
- Highlights correctly classified and misclassified samples, offering insights for improvement.

Real-Life Project:

Project Name: Sentiment Analysis on IMDB Reviews

Project Goal: Train a sentiment analysis model to classify IMDB reviews as positive or negative.

Code for This Project:
```
from fastai.text.all import *
# Load dataset
path = untar_data(URLs.IMDB_SAMPLE)
# Define DataBlock
dblock = DataBlock(
    blocks=(TextBlock.from_folder(), CategoryBlock),
    get_y=parent_label,
    splitter=RandomSplitter(valid_pct=0.2)
)
# Create DataLoaders
dls = dblock.dataloaders(path)
# Initialize Learner
learn = text_classifier_learner(dls, AWD_LSTM,
metrics=accuracy)
# Train the Model
learn.fine_tune(5)
# Evaluate Results
learn.show_results(max_n=6)
```
Expected Output:
- Improved accuracy over training epochs.
- Visualization of predictions and misclassifications.
- Trained sentiment analysis model ready for deployment.

Chapter - 17 Building Custom NLP Pipelines with Fastai

Natural language processing (NLP) often requires tailored pipelines to address specific challenges like unique text formats, custom tokenization, or task-specific preprocessing. In this chapter, we explore how to build custom NLP pipelines using Fastai, enabling flexibility in handling diverse datasets and tasks.

Key Characteristics of Custom NLP Pipelines:

- **Flexibility:** Design workflows suited to specific tasks or datasets.
- **Custom Tokenization:** Supports integrating unique tokenization strategies.
- **Advanced Preprocessing:** Enables application-specific cleaning and transformations.
- **Seamless Integration:** Combines custom functions with Fastai's modules.
- **Efficient Batching:** Handles text sequences with padding, truncation, and batching.

Basic Steps for Building Custom NLP Pipelines:

1. **Load and Inspect Data:** Import raw text and labels.
2. **Define Custom Preprocessing:** Implement tailored cleaning and tokenization.
3. **Create a Custom DataBlock:** Integrate preprocessing into Fastai's DataBlock.
4. **Build DataLoaders:** Convert the DataBlock into DataLoaders for training and validation.
5. **Train and Evaluate Models:** Fine-tune models using the custom pipeline.

Syntax Table:

SL No	Function	Syntax/Example	Description
1	Load Data	`pd.read_csv(filepath)`	Reads raw text data from a CSV file.
2	Custom Preprocess	`def preprocess(text):`	Applies tailored text cleaning and

		ing	. . .	transformations.
3	Define Custom Tokenizer	`Tokenizer(tok_func= custom_tokenizer)`	Implements a unique tokenization function.
4	Create DataBlock	`DataBlock(blocks, get_items, splitter, ...)`	Integrates custom preprocessing into the pipeline.
5	Fine-Tune the Model	`text_classifier_lea rner(dls, AWD_LSTM, metrics)`	Initializes and fine-tunes the model.

Syntax Explanation:

1. Load and Inspect Data

What is Loading and Inspecting Data?

Loading and inspecting data refers to importing raw text data from a file or database into a structured format, such as a Pandas DataFrame. This process also includes examining the dataset's structure and content to ensure it is ready for preprocessing and modeling.

Syntax:

```
import pandas as pd
data = pd.read_csv('dataset.csv')
data.head()
```

Detailed Explanation:

- **Purpose:**
  - o Allows you to load textual datasets stored in external files (e.g., CSV, JSON) into Python.
  - o Provides an initial look at the data to understand its structure (columns, rows) and content.
- **Parameters:**
  - o `filepath`: Path to the CSV file containing text and labels.
- **Steps:**
  - o Reads the CSV file using Pandas.
  - o Displays the first few rows of the dataset using `.head()`.
- **Output:**
  - o A Pandas DataFrame containing text and associated labels for NLP tasks.

Example:
```
data = pd.read_csv('reviews.csv')
data.head()
```
Example Explanation:
- Loads a dataset of reviews and their sentiment labels from a file named `reviews.csv`.
- Displays the first five rows to verify the presence of text and labels in appropriate columns.

2. Define Custom Preprocessing

What is Custom Preprocessing?

Custom preprocessing involves applying specific text cleaning steps to raw data to prepare it for tokenization and modeling. This process might include converting text to lowercase, removing unwanted characters, or normalizing whitespace.

Syntax:
```
def preprocess(text):
    text = text.lower()
    text = re.sub(r'[^a-z0-9\s]', '', text)
    return text
```

Detailed Explanation:
- **Purpose:** Cleans raw text data by removing noise and standardizing it for consistent processing.
- **Parameters:**
  - `text`: A single string of raw text that needs preprocessing.
- **Steps:**
  - Converts all characters in the text to lowercase to ensure uniformity.
  - Removes special characters and punctuation using regular expressions.
  - Returns the cleaned string.
- **Output:** A preprocessed version of the input text, free from unnecessary elements.

Example:
```
cleaned_text = preprocess("Fastai simplifies NLP tasks! ☺")
print(cleaned_text)
```

Example Explanation:

- Input text "Fastai simplifies NLP tasks! ☺" is cleaned to "fastai simplifies nlp tasks".
- The result is suitable for subsequent tokenization and numericalization.

3. Define Custom Tokenizer

What is a Custom Tokenizer?

A custom tokenizer splits text into meaningful units (tokens) based on specific rules or strategies, allowing for task-specific tokenization.

Syntax:

```
def custom_tokenizer(text):
    return text.split()
tokenizer = Tokenizer(tok_func=custom_tokenizer)
```

Detailed Explanation:

- **Purpose:** Allows the use of custom logic for dividing text into tokens, such as splitting on spaces, handling compound words, or using specific delimiters.
- **Parameters:**
    - text: The raw or cleaned text string to be tokenized.
- **Steps:**
    - Implements a function (custom_tokenizer) that defines the rules for tokenization.
    - Integrates this function with Fastai's Tokenizer class.
- **Output:** A list of tokens extracted from the input text.

Example:

```
tokens = custom_tokenizer("Fastai is great for NLP
tasks.")
print(tokens)
```

Example Explanation:

- Splits the sentence "Fastai is great for NLP tasks." into tokens: ['Fastai', 'is', 'great', 'for', 'NLP', 'tasks.'].
- Prepares the text for numericalization and model input.

4. Create DataBlock

What is Creating a DataBlock?

Creating a DataBlock involves defining a modular pipeline for processing text data, integrating all preprocessing, tokenization, and splitting steps.

Syntax:

```
dblock = DataBlock(
    blocks=(TextBlock.from_df('text', seq_len=72),
CategoryBlock),
    get_y=ColReader('label'),
    splitter=RandomSplitter(valid_pct=0.2)
)
```

Detailed Explanation:

- **Purpose:** Specifies how text data and labels are extracted, processed, and split for model training and validation.
- **Parameters:**
  - `TextBlock.from_df`: Defines text data preprocessing and tokenization from a specified column in a DataFrame.
  - `CategoryBlock`: Handles target variables as categorical labels.
  - `get_y`: Extracts labels using a column reader function (e.g., `ColReader('label')`).
  - `splitter`: Divides data into training and validation sets, reserving 20% for validation.
- **Output:** A DataBlock object ready for conversion into DataLoaders.

Example:

```
dblock = DataBlock(
    blocks=(TextBlock.from_df('review', seq_len=100),
CategoryBlock),
    get_y=ColReader('sentiment'),
    splitter=RandomSplitter(valid_pct=0.2)
)
```

Example Explanation:

- Processes text data from the `review` column and sentiment labels from the `sentiment` column.
- Configures the pipeline to tokenize, numericalize, and split the

data.

5. Fine-Tune the Model

What is Fine-Tuning the Model?

Fine-tuning the model adapts a pretrained language model to the specific task defined by the custom pipeline.

Syntax:

```
learn = text_classifier_learner(dls, AWD_LSTM,
metrics=accuracy)
learn.fine_tune(5)
```

Detailed Explanation:

- **Purpose:** Uses transfer learning to train a text classifier on the processed dataset.
- **Parameters:**
  - dls: DataLoaders created from the custom DataBlock.
  - AWD_LSTM: A pretrained model designed for text data.
  - metrics: Metrics like accuracy to evaluate performance during training.
- **Output:** A fine-tuned model ready for prediction tasks.

Example:

```
learn = text_classifier_learner(dls, AWD_LSTM,
metrics=accuracy)
learn.fine_tune(5)
```

Example Explanation:

- Initializes the learner with the custom pipeline's DataLoaders and the AWD-LSTM model.
- Trains the model for 5 epochs, adapting it to classify text into categories based on the labels provided.

Real-Life Project:

Project Name: Custom Sentiment Analysis Pipeline

Project Goal: Build a custom pipeline to classify product reviews as positive or negative.

Code for This Project:

```
from fastai.text.all import *
import pandas as pd
# Load dataset
data = pd.read_csv('reviews.csv')
```

```
# Preprocess text
def preprocess(text):
    text = text.lower()
    text = re.sub(r'[^a-z0-9\s]', '', text)
    return text
data['review'] = data['review'].apply(preprocess)
# Define DataBlock
dblock = DataBlock(
    blocks=(TextBlock.from_df('review', seq_len=100),
CategoryBlock),
    get_y=ColReader('sentiment'),
    splitter=RandomSplitter(valid_pct=0.2)
)
# Create DataLoaders
dls = dblock.dataloaders(data)
# Initialize and Train Model
learn = text_classifier_learner(dls, AWD_LSTM,
metrics=accuracy)
learn.fine_tune(5)
# Evaluate Results
learn.show_results(max_n=6)
```

Expected Output:

- A custom pipeline for preprocessing, tokenizing, and batching text data.
- Improved accuracy on sentiment classification.
- Predictions and misclassifications for further analysis.

Chapter - 18 Working with Tabular Data in Fastai

Tabular data is among the most common types of data in real-world applications, encompassing structured datasets like spreadsheets or relational databases. Fastai's tabular module provides tools for preprocessing, feature engineering, and building machine learning models tailored to tabular data. This chapter explores how to load, preprocess, and model tabular data using Fastai.

Key Characteristics of Tabular Data in Fastai:

- **Flexible Data Preprocessing:** Handles missing values, categorical encoding, and normalization.
- **Feature Engineering:** Supports continuous and categorical variable handling.
- **Integrated DataBlocks:** Simplifies defining workflows for training and validation.
- **Model Optimization:** Leverages neural networks for tabular data.
- **Metrics Tracking:** Provides built-in metrics for performance evaluation.

Basic Steps for Working with Tabular Data:

1. **Load the Dataset:** Import structured data from files or databases.
2. **Define Preprocessing Steps:** Handle missing values, encode categories, and normalize continuous variables.
3. **Create a DataBlock:** Specify inputs, outputs, and transformations.
4. **Build DataLoaders:** Convert the DataBlock into DataLoaders for model training.
5. **Train and Evaluate Models:** Train models and assess performance.

Syntax Table:

SL No	Function	Syntax/Example	Description
1	Load Dataset	`pd.read_csv(filepath)`	Reads structured data from a CSV file.
2	Define DataBlock	`TabularDataBlock(cat_names, cont_names, ...)`	Configures preprocessing for tabular data.
3	Create	`dblock.dataloaders`	Converts DataBlock

		DataLoaders	`(df, ...)`	into DataLoaders.
4	Initialize Tabular Learner	`tabular_learner(dl s, ...)`	Creates a learner for tabular data.
5	Train and Evaluate the Model	`learn.fit_one_cycl e(...)`	Trains the model and evaluates performance.

Syntax Explanation:

1. Load Dataset

What is Loading a Dataset?

Loading a dataset involves importing structured data into a Pandas DataFrame for exploration and preprocessing.

Syntax:

```
import pandas as pd
data = pd.read_csv('dataset.csv')
data.head()
```

Detailed Explanation:

- **Purpose:** Reads tabular data stored in CSV files into Python for further processing.
- **Parameters:**
    - ○ `filepath`: Path to the CSV file containing tabular data.
- **Output:** A Pandas DataFrame with the first few rows displayed for inspection.

Example:

```
data = pd.read_csv('housing.csv')
data.head()
```

Example Explanation:

- Loads a housing dataset with columns like price, size, and location.
- Displays the first five rows to understand the structure and content of the data.

2. Define DataBlock

What is a Tabular DataBlock?

A Tabular DataBlock defines the workflow for preprocessing and handling tabular data, specifying categorical and continuous variables.

Syntax:

```
dblock = TabularDataBlock(
    cat_names=['region', 'type'],
    cont_names=['price', 'size'],
    y_names='price',
    y_block=RegressionBlock(),
    splits=splits
)
```

Detailed Explanation:

- **Purpose:** Sets up a processing pipeline for tabular data, handling categorical encoding, normalization, and splitting.
- **Parameters:**
  - cat_names: List of categorical column names.
  - cont_names: List of continuous column names.
  - y_names: Target variable for prediction.
  - y_block: Specifies the type of prediction (e.g., regression or classification).
  - splits: Indices for training and validation splits.
- **Output:** A configured TabularDataBlock ready to create DataLoaders.

Example:

```
dblock = TabularDataBlock(
    cat_names=['region', 'type'],
    cont_names=['size'],
    y_names='price',
    y_block=RegressionBlock(),
    splits=splits
)
```

Example Explanation:

- Configures a regression task to predict price based on categorical (region, type) and continuous (size) features.
- Uses predefined splits for training and validation.

3. Create DataLoaders

What are Tabular DataLoaders?
Tabular DataLoaders manage batching, preprocessing, and feeding data into the model during training and validation.
Syntax:
```
dls = dblock.dataloaders(df)
```
Detailed Explanation:
- **Purpose:** Converts the TabularDataBlock into DataLoaders for efficient data handling.
- **Parameters:**
    - df: DataFrame containing the dataset.
- **Output:** Training and validation DataLoaders.

Example:
```
dls = dblock.dataloaders(data)
dls.show_batch()
```
Example Explanation:
- Creates DataLoaders for the data DataFrame.
- Displays a batch of processed data to verify correctness.

4. Initialize Tabular Learner

What is a Tabular Learner?
A Tabular Learner is a model designed to handle tabular data, incorporating preprocessing and neural network layers.
Syntax:
```
learn = tabular_learner(dls, layers=[200, 100],
metrics=rmse)
```
Detailed Explanation:
- **Purpose:** Initializes a neural network tailored for tabular data.
- **Parameters:**
    - dls: DataLoaders created from the TabularDataBlock.
    - layers: Defines the architecture of the neural network with two layers of 200 and 100 neurons, respectively.
    - metrics: Evaluation metric(s) such as RMSE (Root Mean Square Error).
- **Output:** A learner object ready for training.

Example:
```
learn = tabular_learner(dls, layers=[300, 150],
metrics=rmse)
```
Example Explanation:
- Creates a model with two hidden layers (300 and 150 neurons).
- Uses RMSE to evaluate performance during training.

5. Train and Evaluate the Model
What is Training and Evaluating the Model?
Training adjusts model weights to minimize error, while evaluation assesses performance on validation data.
Syntax:
```
learn.fit_one_cycle(5, lr=1e-3)
```
Detailed Explanation:
- **Purpose:** Trains the model using a cyclic learning rate policy and evaluates its performance.
- **Parameters:**
  - 5: Number of training epochs.
  - lr=1e-3: Learning rate for optimization.
- **Output:** Training and validation metrics (e.g., RMSE) after each epoch.

Example:
```
learn.fit_one_cycle(10, lr=3e-3)
```
Example Explanation:
- Trains the model for 10 epochs with a learning rate of 0.003.
- Outputs training and validation RMSE for each epoch.

Real-Life Project:
Project Name: Predicting Housing Prices
Project Goal: Build a model to predict house prices based on features like location, type, and size.
Code for This Project:
```
from fastai.tabular.all import *
import pandas as pd

# Load dataset
```

```python
data = pd.read_csv('housing.csv')

# Split dataset
splits = RandomSplitter(valid_pct=0.2)(range_of(data))

# Define DataBlock
dblock = TabularDataBlock(
    cat_names=['region', 'type'],
    cont_names=['size'],
    y_names='price',
    y_block=RegressionBlock(),
    splits=splits
)

# Create DataLoaders
dls = dblock.dataloaders(data)

# Initialize Learner
learn = tabular_learner(dls, layers=[200, 100],
metrics=rmse)

# Train the Model
learn.fit_one_cycle(10, lr=1e-2)

# Evaluate Results
learn.show_results()
```
Expected Output:
- Training and validation RMSE over 10 epochs.
- Predictions and actual values displayed for validation samples.
- Trained model ready for deployment.

Chapter - 19 Handling Categorical and Continuous Features in Fastai

When working with tabular data, handling categorical and continuous features effectively is critical for building accurate and efficient models. Fastai provides built-in support for preprocessing and encoding categorical features, normalizing continuous features, and combining them seamlessly into a pipeline. This chapter covers how to process these feature types for machine learning tasks using Fastai.

Key Characteristics of Feature Handling in Fastai:

- **Categorical Encoding:** Converts categorical variables into numerical representations.
- **Continuous Normalization:** Normalizes continuous variables for consistent scaling.
- **Automatic Preprocessing:** Integrates feature handling into DataBlocks and DataLoaders.
- **Feature Importance:** Evaluates the importance of features for model predictions.

Basic Steps for Handling Features:

1. **Identify Feature Types:** Separate features into categorical and continuous groups.
2. **Define Preprocessing Steps:** Encode categorical features and normalize continuous ones.
3. **Integrate with DataBlock:** Specify feature handling in a TabularDataBlock.
4. **Train and Evaluate Models:** Use the processed features for training.
5. **Analyze Feature Importance:** Interpret the contribution of features to predictions.

Syntax Table:

SL No	Function	Syntax/Example	Description
1	Define Categorical Features	`cat_names = ['region', 'type']`	Lists the names of categorical columns.
2	Define	`cont_names =`	Lists the names of

	Continuous Features	`['price', 'size']`	continuous columns.
3	Create DataBlock	`TabularDataBlock(c at_names, cont_names, ...)`	Configures preprocessing for feature types.
4	Analyze Feature Importance	`learn.show_importa nce(...)`	Displays feature importance.

Syntax Explanation:

1. Define Categorical Features

What are Categorical Features?

Categorical features are variables with a fixed number of discrete categories or levels, such as `region` or `type` in a dataset.

Syntax:

`cat_names = ['region', 'type']`

Detailed Explanation:

- **Purpose:** Identifies columns in the dataset that contain categorical data.
- **How it Works:**
    - Categorical data will be automatically encoded into numerical values during preprocessing.
    - Encoding ensures models can interpret and use these variables effectively.
- **Output:** A list of column names representing categorical features.

Example:

`cat_names = ['region', 'type']`

Example Explanation:

- Defines `region` and `type` as categorical features.
- Prepares these columns for encoding during model training.

2. Define Continuous Features

What are Continuous Features?

Continuous features are numerical variables that can take on any value within a range, such as `price` or `size`.

Syntax:

`cont_names = ['price', 'size']`

Detailed Explanation:

- **Purpose:** Identifies columns containing continuous numerical data.
- **How it Works:**
  - Continuous features are normalized (scaled) to ensure uniform input ranges for the model.
  - Normalization improves model performance and convergence during training.
- **Output:** A list of column names representing continuous features.

Example:
```
cont_names = ['price', 'size']
```
Example Explanation:
- Identifies price and size as continuous features in the dataset.
- Ensures these features are scaled appropriately for model input.

3. Create DataBlock
What is a Tabular DataBlock?
A Tabular DataBlock specifies how to process categorical and continuous features and integrate them into a machine learning pipeline.

Syntax:
```
dblock = TabularDataBlock(
    cat_names=cat_names,
    cont_names=cont_names,
    y_names='price',
    y_block=RegressionBlock(),
    splits=splits
)
```
Detailed Explanation:
- **Purpose:** Preprocesses and combines categorical and continuous features into a single pipeline.
- **Parameters:**
  - cat_names: List of categorical features to encode.
  - cont_names: List of continuous features to normalize.
  - y_names: Target variable for prediction.
  - y_block: Specifies the prediction task type (e.g., regression or classification).
  - splits: Defines training and validation splits.

- **Output:** A DataBlock object ready to create DataLoaders.

Example:

```
dblock = TabularDataBlock(
    cat_names=['region', 'type'],
    cont_names=['size'],
    y_names='price',
    y_block=RegressionBlock(),
    splits=splits
)
```

Example Explanation:

- Configures a regression task using `region` and `type` as categorical features and `size` as a continuous feature.
- Prepares the dataset for training and validation.

4. Analyze Feature Importance

What is Feature Importance?

Feature importance quantifies the contribution of each feature to the model's predictions.

Syntax:

```
learn.show_importance()
```

Detailed Explanation:

- **Purpose:** Identifies which features have the most impact on the model's performance.
- **How it Works:**
  - Calculates importance scores for all features based on their effect on predictions.
  - Helps identify and prioritize key variables for decision-making.
- **Output:** A visual or tabular representation of feature importance.

Example:

```
learn.show_importance()
```

Example Explanation:

- Displays a ranked list of features by their importance in influencing model predictions.
- Provides insights for feature engineering and model refinement.

Real-Life Project:

Project Name: Feature Engineering for Housing Price Prediction

Project Goal: Process and analyze features to predict house prices effectively.

Code for This Project:

```python
from fastai.tabular.all import *
import pandas as pd
# Load dataset
data = pd.read_csv('housing.csv')
# Split dataset
splits = RandomSplitter(valid_pct=0.2)(range_of(data))
# Define features
cat_names = ['region', 'type']
cont_names = ['size']
# Define DataBlock
dblock = TabularDataBlock(
    cat_names=cat_names,
    cont_names=cont_names,
    y_names='price',
    y_block=RegressionBlock(),
    splits=splits
)
# Create DataLoaders
dls = dblock.dataloaders(data)
# Initialize Learner
learn = tabular_learner(dls, layers=[200, 100],
metrics=rmse)
# Train the Model
learn.fit_one_cycle(10, lr=1e-2)

# Evaluate Feature Importance
learn.show_importance()
```

Expected Output:

- Training and validation RMSE over 10 epochs.
- Feature importance ranked by contribution to predictions.
- Insights for refining feature engineering.

Chapter - 20 Feature Engineering for Tabular Models in Fastai

Feature engineering is the process of transforming raw data into meaningful input for machine learning models. For tabular data, it involves handling missing values, creating new features, scaling data, and encoding categorical variables. Fastai simplifies feature engineering by integrating these steps into its tabular data pipeline. This chapter explores effective techniques for feature engineering with Fastai.

Key Characteristics of Feature Engineering in Fastai:

- **Feature Creation:** Generates new features from existing ones, such as interaction terms.
  Missing Value Handling: Imputes missing values for continuous and categorical data.
- **Scaling and Normalization:** Applies transformations to continuous variables for consistent ranges.
- **Encoding Categorical Variables:** Maps categories to numeric values using embedding techniques.
- **Built-In Transformations:** Automates preprocessing with minimal code.

Basic Steps for Feature Engineering:

1. **Analyze Raw Data:** Inspect and understand the structure and quality of the dataset.
2. **Handle Missing Values:** Impute missing entries with appropriate strategies.
3. **Create New Features:** Derive meaningful features to enhance model learning.
4. **Scale and Normalize:** Standardize continuous variables to improve model performance.
5. **Encode Categorical Features:** Map categories to numerical representations.
6. **Integrate into DataBlock:** Use Fastai's TabularDataBlock for seamless feature integration.

Syntax Table:

SL No	Function	Syntax/Example	Description
1	Handle Missing Values	`FillMissing()`	Fills missing values for continuous variables.
2	Create Interaction Features	`df['new_feature'] = df['A'] * df['B']`	Creates a new feature from existing ones.
3	Normalize Continuous Features	`Normalize()`	Scales continuous variables to a uniform range.
4	Encode Categorical Variables	`Categorify()`	Converts categories to numerical indices.
5	Integrate Transformations	`TabularDataBlock(...)`	Combines all preprocessing steps into a pipeline.

Syntax Explanation:

1. Handle Missing Values

What is Handling Missing Values?

Handling missing values involves filling gaps in the dataset to ensure all rows have complete information. Missing continuous variables are imputed using their median, while categorical variables are replaced with a placeholder value, ensuring the data remains valid for model training.

Syntax:

`FillMissing(add_col=True)`

Detailed Explanation:

- **Purpose:** Addresses incomplete data to avoid errors during model training and improve model accuracy.
- **Parameters:**
  - add_col: If set to True, creates an additional column for each continuous variable to indicate whether its value was originally missing.
- **Steps:**
  - Continuous variables are filled with their median value.
  - Placeholder categories are assigned to missing categorical

values.

- **Output:** A dataset without missing values in the specified columns.

Example:
```
from fastai.tabular.all import *
procs = [FillMissing()]
```
Example Explanation:

- Uses the `FillMissing` processor to fill gaps in continuous variables with their median values.
- Adds an indicator column for each continuous variable that originally had missing values, enabling analysis of how missingness affects predictions.

2. Create Interaction Features

What are Interaction Features?

Interaction features represent the relationship between two or more variables by combining them mathematically. This technique captures higher-order interactions that might be useful for predictions.

Syntax:
```
df['new_feature'] = df['A'] * df['B']
```
Detailed Explanation:

- **Purpose:** Adds new dimensions to the dataset by deriving features that highlight relationships between existing variables.
- **Steps:**
  - Choose relevant columns (A and B) for interaction.
  - Apply an operation, such as multiplication or division, to create the interaction feature.
  - Store the result in a new column.
- **Output:** A dataset with an additional column representing the interaction.

Example:
```
data['interaction'] = data['size'] * data['price']
```

Example Explanation:

- Computes a new feature, `interaction`, by multiplying the `size` and `price` columns.

- Captures the combined effect of size and price, potentially improving the model's ability to predict target variables.

3. Normalize Continuous Features

What is Normalizing Continuous Features?

Normalization ensures that all continuous features have the same scale, with a mean of 0 and a standard deviation of 1. This standardization helps models converge faster during training and prevents any single feature from dominating due to its scale.

Syntax:

```
Normalize()
```

Detailed Explanation:

- **Purpose:** Standardizes continuous variables to eliminate differences in scale.
- **Steps:**
  - For each continuous column, subtract the mean and divide by the standard deviation.
- **Output:** Normalized continuous features suitable for machine learning algorithms.

Example:

```
procs = [Normalize()]
```

Example Explanation:

- Applies the Normalize processor to all continuous columns.
- Ensures each feature has a mean of 0 and a standard deviation of 1, improving model stability and training speed.

4. Encode Categorical Variables

What is Encoding Categorical Variables?

Encoding categorical variables converts categories into numerical representations, enabling models to interpret them. Each unique category is assigned a unique integer value.

Syntax:

```
Categorify()
```

Detailed Explanation:

- **Purpose:** Transforms string-based categories into numerical indices.
- **Steps:**

o   Maps each unique value in a categorical column to a unique integer.
- **Output:** A dataset where all categorical columns are represented numerically.

Example:
```
procs = [Categorify()]
```
Example Explanation:
- Replaces each category in a column with its corresponding integer index.
- Allows the model to treat categorical data numerically during training.

5. Integrate Transformations into DataBlock

What is Integrating Transformations?

Integrating transformations into a DataBlock combines all preprocessing steps into a single pipeline, ensuring that categorical and continuous features are handled seamlessly.

Syntax:
```
dblock = TabularDataBlock(
    cat_names=['region', 'type'],
    cont_names=['size'],
    y_names='price',
    procs=[Categorify, FillMissing, Normalize()],
    splits=splits
)
```

Detailed Explanation:
- **Purpose:** Streamlines the preprocessing workflow by combining encoding, normalization, and missing value handling.
- **Parameters:**
    o   cat_names: Specifies columns containing categorical data.
    o   cont_names: Specifies columns containing continuous data.
    o   y_names: Specifies the target variable for prediction.
    o   procs: Lists preprocessing functions to apply.
    o   splits: Defines training and validation data splits.

- **Output:** A TabularDataBlock ready to be converted into DataLoaders.

Example:
```
dblock = TabularDataBlock(
    cat_names=['region', 'type'],
    cont_names=['size'],
    y_names='price',
    procs=[Categorify, FillMissing, Normalize()],
    splits=splits
)
```

Example Explanation:
- Configures a pipeline that processes categorical and continuous features, handles missing values, and normalizes data in preparation for training.
- Encodes region and type as categorical features and normalizes size as a continuous feature.

Real-Life Project:

Project Name: Feature Engineering for Loan Approval Prediction

Project Goal: Use feature engineering techniques to improve predictions for loan approval based on applicant data.

Code for This Project:
```
from fastai.tabular.all import *
import pandas as pd

# Load dataset
data = pd.read_csv('loans.csv')

# Split dataset
splits = RandomSplitter(valid_pct=0.2)(range_of(data))

# Define features
cat_names = ['gender', 'education', 'marital_status']
cont_names = ['income', 'loan_amount']

# Define DataBlock
dblock = TabularDataBlock(
```

```
    cat_names=cat_names,
    cont_names=cont_names,
    y_names='approved',
    procs=[Categorify, FillMissing, Normalize()],
    splits=splits
)

# Create DataLoaders
dls = dblock.dataloaders(data)

# Initialize Learner
learn = tabular_learner(dls, layers=[100, 50],
metrics=accuracy)

# Train the Model
learn.fit_one_cycle(5, lr=1e-2)

# Evaluate Results
learn.show_results()
```
Expected Output:
- Improved accuracy over multiple epochs.
- Preprocessed data ready for efficient model training.
- Insights into feature contributions for loan approval.

Chapter - 21 Feature Engineering for Tabular Models in Fastai

Feature engineering is the process of transforming raw data into meaningful input for machine learning models. For tabular data, it involves handling missing values, creating new features, scaling data, and encoding categorical variables. Fastai simplifies feature engineering by integrating these steps into its tabular data pipeline. This chapter explores effective techniques for feature engineering with Fastai.

Key Characteristics of Feature Engineering in Fastai:

- **Feature Creation:** Generates new features from existing ones, such as interaction terms.
- **Missing Value Handling:** Imputes missing values for continuous and categorical data.
- **Scaling and Normalization:** Applies transformations to continuous variables for consistent ranges.
- **Encoding Categorical Variables:** Maps categories to numeric values using embedding techniques.
- **Built-In Transformations:** Automates preprocessing with minimal code.

Basic Steps for Feature Engineering:

1. **Analyze Raw Data:** Inspect and understand the structure and quality of the dataset.
2. **Handle Missing Values:** Impute missing entries with appropriate strategies.
3. **Create New Features:** Derive meaningful features to enhance model learning.
4. **Scale and Normalize:** Standardize continuous variables to improve model performance.
5. **Encode Categorical Features:** Map categories to numerical representations.
6. **Integrate into DataBlock:** Use Fastai's TabularDataBlock for seamless feature integration.

Syntax Table:

SL No	Function	Syntax/Example	Description

1	Handle Missing Values	`FillMissing()`	Fills missing values for continuous variables.
2	Create Interaction Features	`df['new_feature'] = df['A'] * df['B']`	Creates a new feature from existing ones.
3	Normalize Continuous Features	`Normalize()`	Scales continuous variables to a uniform range.
4	Encode Categorical Variables	`Categorify()`	Converts categories to numerical indices.
5	Integrate Transformations	`TabularDataBlock(...)`	Combines all preprocessing steps into a pipeline.

Syntax Explanation:

1. Handle Missing Values
What is Handling Missing Values?
Handling missing values involves filling gaps in the dataset to ensure all rows have complete information. Missing continuous variables are imputed using their median, while categorical variables are replaced with a placeholder value, ensuring the data remains valid for model training.
Syntax:
`FillMissing(add_col=True)`
Detailed Explanation:
- **Purpose:** Addresses incomplete data to avoid errors during model training and improve model accuracy.
- **Parameters:**
    - `add_col`: If set to `True`, creates an additional column for each continuous variable to indicate whether its value was originally missing.
- **Steps:**
    - Continuous variables are filled with their median value.
    - Placeholder categories are assigned to missing categorical values.

- **Output:** A dataset without missing values in the specified columns.

Example:
```
from fastai.tabular.all import *
procs = [FillMissing()]
```
Example Explanation:
- Uses the `FillMissing` processor to fill gaps in continuous variables with their median values.
- Adds an indicator column for each continuous variable that originally had missing values, enabling analysis of how missingness affects predictions.

2. Create Interaction Features

What are Interaction Features?

Interaction features represent the relationship between two or more variables by combining them mathematically. This technique captures higher-order interactions that might be useful for predictions.

Syntax:
```
df['new_feature'] = df['A'] * df['B']
```
Detailed Explanation:
- **Purpose:** Adds new dimensions to the dataset by deriving features that highlight relationships between existing variables.
- **Steps:**
  - Choose relevant columns (A and B) for interaction.
  - Apply an operation, such as multiplication or division, to create the interaction feature.
  - Store the result in a new column.
- **Output:** A dataset with an additional column representing the interaction.

Example:
```
data['interaction'] = data['size'] * data['price']
```
Example Explanation:
- Computes a new feature, `interaction`, by multiplying the `size` and `price` columns.
- Captures the combined effect of size and price, potentially improving the model's ability to predict target variables.

3. Normalize Continuous Features

What is Normalizing Continuous Features?

Normalization ensures that all continuous features have the same scale, with a mean of 0 and a standard deviation of 1. This standardization helps models converge faster during training and prevents any single feature from dominating due to its scale.

Syntax:

```
Normalize()
```

Detailed Explanation:

- **Purpose:** Standardizes continuous variables to eliminate differences in scale.
- **Steps:**
  - For each continuous column, subtract the mean and divide by the standard deviation.
- **Output:** Normalized continuous features suitable for machine learning algorithms.

Example:

```
procs = [Normalize()]
```

Example Explanation:

- Applies the `Normalize` processor to all continuous columns.
- Ensures each feature has a mean of 0 and a standard deviation of 1, improving model stability and training speed.

4. Encode Categorical Variables

What is Encoding Categorical Variables?

Encoding categorical variables converts categories into numerical representations, enabling models to interpret them. Each unique category is assigned a unique integer value.

Syntax:

```
Categorify()
```

Detailed Explanation:

- **Purpose:** Transforms string-based categories into numerical indices.
- **Steps:**
  - Maps each unique value in a categorical column to a unique integer.
- **Output:** A dataset where all categorical columns are represented

numerically.

Example:
```
procs = [Categorify()]
```

Example Explanation:
- Replaces each category in a column with its corresponding integer index.
- Allows the model to treat categorical data numerically during training.

5. Integrate Transformations into DataBlock

What is Integrating Transformations?

Integrating transformations into a DataBlock combines all preprocessing steps into a single pipeline, ensuring that categorical and continuous features are handled seamlessly.

Syntax:
```
dblock = TabularDataBlock(
    cat_names=['region', 'type'],
    cont_names=['size'],
    y_names='price',
    procs=[Categorify, FillMissing, Normalize()],
    splits=splits
)
```

Detailed Explanation:
- **Purpose:** Streamlines the preprocessing workflow by combining encoding, normalization, and missing value handling.
- **Parameters:**
    - cat_names: Specifies columns containing categorical data.
    - cont_names: Specifies columns containing continuous data.
    - y_names: Specifies the target variable for prediction.
    - procs: Lists preprocessing functions to apply.
    - splits: Defines training and validation data splits.
- **Output:** A TabularDataBlock ready to be converted into DataLoaders.

Example:

```
dblock = TabularDataBlock(
    cat_names=['region', 'type'],
    cont_names=['size'],
    y_names='price',
    procs=[Categorify, FillMissing, Normalize()],
    splits=splits
)
```

Example Explanation:

- Configures a pipeline that processes categorical and continuous features, handles missing values, and normalizes data in preparation for training.
- Encodes region and type as categorical features and normalizes size as a continuous feature.

Real-Life Project:

Project Name: Feature Engineering for Loan Approval Prediction

Project Goal: Use feature engineering techniques to improve predictions for loan approval based on applicant data.

Code for This Project:

```
from fastai.tabular.all import *
import pandas as pd
# Load dataset
data = pd.read_csv('loans.csv')
# Split dataset
splits = RandomSplitter(valid_pct=0.2)(range_of(data))
# Define features
cat_names = ['gender', 'education', 'marital_status']
cont_names = ['income', 'loan_amount']

# Define DataBlock
dblock = TabularDataBlock(
    cat_names=cat_names,
    cont_names=cont_names,
    y_names='approved',
    procs=[Categorify, FillMissing, Normalize()],
    splits=splits
)
```

```
# Create DataLoaders
dls = dblock.dataloaders(data)
# Initialize Learner
learn = tabular_learner(dls, layers=[100, 50],
metrics=accuracy)
# Train the Model
learn.fit_one_cycle(5, lr=1e-2)
# Evaluate Results
learn.show_results()
```

Expected Output:
- Improved accuracy over multiple epochs.
- Preprocessed data ready for efficient model training.
- Insights into feature contributions for loan approval.

Chapter - 22 Interpreting Tabular Model Outputs in Fastai

Interpreting model outputs is a crucial step in understanding and improving the performance of tabular models. Fastai provides tools to interpret predictions, evaluate feature importance, and analyze model performance, helping users gain insights into how the model makes decisions. This chapter focuses on techniques to interpret tabular model outputs effectively.

Key Characteristics of Model Interpretation in Fastai:

- **Prediction Analysis:** Examines individual and batch predictions.
- **Feature Importance:** Identifies features that contribute most to model decisions.
- **Error Analysis:** Detects patterns in misclassified or poorly predicted samples.
- **SHAP Values:** Uses SHAP (SHapley Additive exPlanations) for local and global interpretation.

Basic Steps for Interpreting Tabular Model Outputs:

1. **Examine Predictions:** Inspect individual predictions to verify correctness.
2. **Visualize Feature Importance:** Identify key features influencing predictions.
3. **Analyze Errors:** Investigate incorrect predictions to improve data quality or model performance.
4. **Apply SHAP Values:** Use SHAP for detailed interpretation of model behavior.

Syntax Table:

SL No	Function	Syntax/Example	Description
1	Show Predictions	`learn.show_results()`	Displays predictions alongside actual values.
2	Feature Importance	`learn.show_importance(...)`	Displays feature importance rankings.

3	Get Prediction Probabilities	`learn.get_pr eds()`	Fetches probabilities for predictions.
4	Interpret with SHAP	`learn.interp ret()`	Generates SHAP values for interpretation.

Syntax Explanation:

1. Show Predictions

What is Showing Predictions?

Displaying predictions alongside actual values helps verify the model's performance and identify patterns in correct or incorrect predictions.

Syntax:

```
learn.show_results(max_n=10)
```

Detailed Explanation:

- **Purpose:** Visualizes how well the model performs on a batch of validation data.
- **Parameters:**
  - max_n: Specifies the number of predictions to display.
- **Output:** A table showing input features, actual target values, and predicted values.

Example:

```
learn.show_results(max_n=5)
```

Example Explanation:

- Displays predictions for five validation samples, highlighting areas where the model performs well or struggles.
- Helps users identify misclassifications or unusual patterns in predictions.

2. Feature Importance

What is Feature Importance?

Feature importance identifies which features contribute most significantly to the model's predictions, providing insights into the model's decision-making process.

Syntax:

```
learn.show_importance()
```

Detailed Explanation:

- **Purpose:** Ranks features based on their influence on model predictions.
- **How it Works:**

- - Calculates scores for each feature based on their impact on the model's output.
  - Displays a ranked list or visualization of feature importance.
- **Output:** A bar chart or table showing feature importance scores.

Example:

```
learn.show_importance()
```

Example Explanation:
- Highlights the most critical features affecting predictions, such as income or age.
- Helps users focus on refining the most impactful variables.

3. Get Prediction Probabilities
What is Fetching Prediction Probabilities?
Fetching prediction probabilities provides detailed confidence scores for each prediction, aiding in uncertainty analysis and decision-making.

Syntax:

```
preds, targets = learn.get_preds()
```

Detailed Explanation:
- **Purpose:** Retrieves raw prediction probabilities and true labels for analysis.
- **Parameters:**
  - None required for default behavior.
- **Output:** Two arrays: one for prediction probabilities and another for corresponding true labels.

Example:

```
preds, targets = learn.get_preds()
print(preds[:5], targets[:5])
```

Example Explanation:
- Displays the first five prediction probabilities and their corresponding true labels.
- Allows users to assess the model's confidence in its predictions.

4. Interpret with SHAP
What is SHAP Interpretation?
SHAP values provide local and global explanations for model predictions,

showing how individual features impact predictions.

Syntax:

```
learn.interpret()
```

Detailed Explanation:

- **Purpose:** Explains model predictions by quantifying the contribution of each feature.
- **How it Works:**
  - ○ Calculates SHAP values for individual samples or the entire dataset.
  - ○ Visualizes feature contributions for better interpretability.
- **Output:** Visualizations such as summary plots, dependence plots, or force plots.

Example:

```
interp = learn.interpret()
interp.plot_feature_importance()
```

Example Explanation:

- Displays a bar chart ranking features by their SHAP value contributions.
- Helps users understand why specific predictions were made.

Real-Life Project:

Project Name: Understanding Customer Churn Predictions

Project Goal: Interpret a classification model for customer churn to identify key drivers of churn and improve business strategies.

Code for This Project:

```
from fastai.tabular.all import *
import pandas as pd
# Load dataset
data = pd.read_csv('customer_churn.csv')
# Split dataset
splits = RandomSplitter(valid_pct=0.2)(range_of(data))
# Define features
cat_names = ['gender', 'region']
cont_names = ['income', 'age']
# Define DataBlock
dblock = TabularDataBlock(
    cat_names=cat_names,
```

```
        cont_names=cont_names,
        y_names='churn',
        y_block=CategoryBlock(),
        procs=[Categorify, FillMissing, Normalize()],
        splits=splits
)
# Create DataLoaders
dls = dblock.dataloaders(data)
# Initialize Learner
learn = tabular_learner(dls, layers=[200, 100],
metrics=accuracy)
# Train the Model
learn.fit_one_cycle(10, lr=1e-2)
# Interpret Results
learn.show_results()
learn.show_importance()
interp = learn.interpret()
interp.plot_feature_importance()
```

Expected Output:

- Predictions displayed alongside actual values for validation samples.
- Ranked feature importance with visualizations.
- SHAP-based feature contribution analysis for specific predictions.

Chapter - 23 Time Series Analysis with Fastai

Time series analysis involves understanding temporal data to forecast future values, detect trends, or identify anomalies. With Fastai, time series tasks can be streamlined using specialized modules for data preparation, feature engineering, and model training. This chapter explores how to perform time series analysis with Fastai.

Key Characteristics of Time Series Analysis in Fastai:

- **Sequential Data Handling:** Supports temporal dependencies in data.
- **Feature Engineering:** Extracts time-based features like lag, rolling statistics, and time of day.
- **Custom DataLoaders:** Prepares sequences with appropriate targets.
- **Modeling Flexibility:** Offers prebuilt architectures or integration with PyTorch models.
- **Evaluation Metrics:** Tracks performance using metrics such as MAE, MSE, and RMSE.

Basic Steps for Time Series Analysis:

1. **Prepare the Dataset:** Organize and inspect temporal data.
2. **Engineer Features:** Create relevant time-based features.
3. **Define DataBlock:** Specify input-output relationships for time series.
4. **Train Models:** Train neural networks or other models to predict future values.
5. **Evaluate Performance:** Analyze model performance using validation data.

Syntax Table:

SL No	Function	Syntax/Example	Description
1	Load Time Series Data	`pd.read_csv(filepath, parse_dates=...)`	Loads time series data from a CSV file.
2	Feature	`df['lag'] =`	Creates lag features

	Engineering	`df['value'].shift(1)`	from the time series.
3	Define DataBlock	`DataBlock(blocks, get_x, get_y, splitter)`	Prepares data for training and validation.
4	Train the Model	`learn.fit_one_cycle(...)`	Trains a model for forecasting.
5	Evaluate the Model	`learn.show_results()`	Displays predictions alongside true values.

Syntax Explanation:

1. Load Time Series Data
What is Loading Time Series Data?
Loading time series data involves importing temporal data from external sources, ensuring the datetime column is properly parsed.
Syntax:
```
import pandas as pd
data = pd.read_csv('time_series.csv',
parse_dates=['date'])
data.head()
```
Detailed Explanation:
- **Purpose:** Reads time series data from a file into a Pandas DataFrame.
- **Parameters:**
  - `filepath`: Path to the CSV file containing the time series data.
  - `parse_dates`: Ensures specified columns are parsed as datetime objects.
- **Output:** A DataFrame with parsed datetime columns and the first few rows displayed for inspection.

Example:
```
data = pd.read_csv('sales_data.csv',
parse_dates=['date'])
data.head()
```

Example Explanation:

- Loads sales data with a `date` column parsed as datetime.
- Ensures the dataset is ready for time-based operations, such as indexing and resampling.

2. Feature Engineering

What is Feature Engineering for Time Series?

Feature engineering creates additional features from the original time series, such as lags, rolling averages, or time-based indicators.

Syntax:

```
data['lag_1'] = data['value'].shift(1)
data['rolling_mean'] =
data['value'].rolling(window=3).mean()
```

Detailed Explanation:

- **Purpose:** Enhances the dataset with derived features to capture temporal patterns.
- **Parameters:**
  - `shift(n)`: Creates lag features by shifting the time series by n steps.
  - `rolling(window)`: Computes rolling statistics over a specified window size.
- **Output:** A DataFrame with additional columns for lagged values and rolling statistics.

Example:

```
data['lag_1'] = data['value'].shift(1)
data['rolling_mean'] =
data['value'].rolling(window=3).mean()
```

Example Explanation:

- Adds a lag feature (`lag_1`) and a rolling mean feature (`rolling_mean`) with a window size of 3.
- Helps capture short-term trends and dependencies in the time series.

3. Define DataBlock

What is a Time Series DataBlock?

A Time Series DataBlock prepares temporal data for training and validation, defining how sequences and targets are generated.

Syntax:

```
dblock = DataBlock(
    blocks=(InputBlock, RegressionBlock),
    get_x=lambda x: x['features'],
    get_y=lambda x: x['target'],
    splitter=RandomSplitter(valid_pct=0.2)
)
```

Detailed Explanation:

- **Purpose:** Configures data processing for time series modeling.
- **Parameters:**
    - blocks: Specifies input and output types (e.g., sequences and regression targets).
    - get_x: Extracts features from the dataset.
    - get_y: Extracts target values from the dataset.
    - splitter: Divides the data into training and validation sets.
- **Output:** A DataBlock ready to create DataLoaders.

Example:

```
dblock = DataBlock(
    blocks=(InputBlock, RegressionBlock),
    get_x=lambda x: x[['lag_1', 'rolling_mean']],
    get_y=lambda x: x['value'],
    splitter=RandomSplitter(valid_pct=0.2)
)
```

Example Explanation:

- Defines lag_1 and rolling_mean as input features and value as the target variable.
- Splits the dataset into training and validation subsets for model training.

4. Train the Model

What is Training the Model?

Training the model involves fitting a neural network to predict target values from input features.

Syntax:

```
learn = tabular_learner(dls, layers=[100, 50],
metrics=rmse)
learn.fit_one_cycle(10, lr=1e-3)
```

Detailed Explanation:

- **Purpose:** Fits a neural network to the training data and evaluates it on validation data.
- **Parameters:**
  - `layers`: Specifies the architecture of the neural network.
  - `metrics`: Evaluation metrics like RMSE for regression tasks.
  - `lr`: Learning rate for optimization.
- **Output:** Trained model and validation metrics.

Example:

```
learn = tabular_learner(dls, layers=[200, 100],
metrics=rmse)
learn.fit_one_cycle(5, lr=3e-3)
```

Example Explanation:

- Trains a model with two hidden layers and monitors RMSE during training.
- Outputs training and validation metrics for each epoch.

5. Evaluate the Model

What is Evaluating the Model?

Evaluation compares the model's predictions against true values to assess performance.

Syntax:

```
learn.show_results()
```

Detailed Explanation:

- **Purpose:** Displays a comparison of predicted and actual values for validation samples.
- **Parameters:**
  - None required for default behavior.
- **Output:** A table showing input features, true values, and predictions.

Example:

```
learn.show_results()
```

Example Explanation:

- Highlights areas where the model performs well or needs improvement.

- Provides insights into prediction accuracy and potential areas for refinement.

Real-Life Project:

Project Name: Forecasting Retail Sales

Project Goal: Build a model to forecast daily sales for a retail store based on historical data.

Code for This Project:

```python
from fastai.tabular.all import *
import pandas as pd
# Load dataset
data = pd.read_csv('retail_sales.csv',
parse_dates=['date'])
data['lag_1'] = data['sales'].shift(1)
data['rolling_mean'] =
data['sales'].rolling(window=7).mean()
data = data.dropna()
# Split dataset
splits = RandomSplitter(valid_pct=0.2)(range_of(data))
# Define DataBlock
dblock = TabularDataBlock(
    blocks=(InputBlock, RegressionBlock),
    get_x=lambda x: x[['lag_1', 'rolling_mean']],
    get_y=lambda x: x['sales'],
    splitter=RandomSplitter(valid_pct=0.2)
)
# Create DataLoaders
dls = dblock.dataloaders(data)
# Initialize Learner
learn = tabular_learner(dls, layers=[200, 100],
metrics=rmse)
# Train the Model
learn.fit_one_cycle(10, lr=1e-2)
# Evaluate Results
learn.show_results()
```

Expected Output:

- Training and validation RMSE over multiple epochs.
- Predictions and actual values displayed for validation samples.

Chapter - 24 Training Models for Forecasting Tasks in Fastai

Forecasting involves predicting future values based on historical data. With Fastai, building forecasting models is straightforward, leveraging tools for feature engineering, sequence modeling, and performance evaluation. This chapter provides a comprehensive guide to training forecasting models with Fastai.

Key Characteristics of Forecasting Models in Fastai:

- **Sequential Data Handling:** Accommodates temporal dependencies in data.
- **Feature Engineering:** Generates time-based features like lags, rolling statistics, and seasonal indicators.
- **Custom DataLoaders:** Manages sequence-to-sequence or sequence-to-value modeling.
- **Prebuilt Architectures:** Supports neural networks tailored for time series forecasting.
- **Metrics Tracking:** Evaluates models with metrics like MAE, MSE, and RMSE.

Basic Steps for Training Forecasting Models:

1. **Prepare the Dataset:** Load and organize temporal data.
2. **Engineer Features:** Create meaningful time-based features.
3. **Define DataBlock:** Specify input-output relationships for forecasting.
4. **Train Models:** Train neural networks or other models to predict future values.
5. **Evaluate Performance:** Assess the model's accuracy and refine as needed.

Syntax Table:

SL No	Function	Syntax/Example	Description
1	Load Time Series Data	`pd.read_csv(filepath, parse_dates=...)`	Loads time series data from a CSV file.
2	Feature Engineering	`df['lag'] = df['value'].shift(1)`	Creates lag features from the time series.

3	Define DataBlock	`DataBlock(blocks, get_x, get_y, splitter)`	Prepares data for training and validation.
4	Train the Model	`learn.fit_one_cycle (...)`	Trains a model for forecasting.
5	Evaluate the Model	`learn.show_results( )`	Displays predictions alongside true values.

Syntax Explanation:

1. Load Time Series Data

What is Loading Time Series Data?

Loading time series data involves importing temporal data from external sources and ensuring the datetime column is properly parsed.

Syntax:

```
import pandas as pd
data = pd.read_csv('time_series.csv',
parse_dates=['date'])
data.head()
```

Detailed Explanation:

- **Purpose:** Reads time series data from a file into a Pandas DataFrame.
- **Parameters:**
  - `filepath`: Path to the CSV file containing the time series data.
  - `parse_dates`: Ensures specified columns are parsed as datetime objects.
- **Output:** A DataFrame with parsed datetime columns and the first few rows displayed for inspection.

Example:

```
data = pd.read_csv('sales_data.csv',
parse_dates=['date'])
data.head()
```

Example Explanation:

- Loads sales data with a `date` column parsed as datetime.
- Ensures the dataset is ready for time-based operations, such as indexing and resampling.

2. Feature Engineering
What is Feature Engineering for Forecasting?
Feature engineering enhances the dataset by deriving features that capture temporal dependencies, such as lags, rolling averages, and time-based indicators.

Syntax:
```
data['lag_1'] = data['value'].shift(1)
data['rolling_mean'] =
data['value'].rolling(window=3).mean()
```
Detailed Explanation:

- **Purpose:** Creates derived features that improve the model's ability to capture temporal patterns.
- **Parameters:**
    - `shift(n)`: Generates lagged features by shifting the time series by n steps.
    - `rolling(window)`: Computes rolling statistics over a specified window size.
- **Output:** A DataFrame with additional columns for lagged values and rolling statistics.

Example:
```
data['lag_1'] = data['value'].shift(1)
data['rolling_mean'] =
data['value'].rolling(window=3).mean()
```

Example Explanation:
- Adds a lag feature (`lag_1`) and a rolling mean feature (`rolling_mean`) with a window size of 3.
- Helps capture short-term trends and dependencies in the time series.

3. Define DataBlock
What is a Forecasting DataBlock?
A Forecasting DataBlock prepares temporal data for training and validation, defining how sequences and targets are generated.

Syntax:

```
dblock = DataBlock(
    blocks=(InputBlock, RegressionBlock),
    get_x=lambda x: x[['features']],
    get_y=lambda x: x['target'],
    splitter=RandomSplitter(valid_pct=0.2)
)
```

Detailed Explanation:

- **Purpose:** Configures data processing for time series forecasting.
- **Parameters:**
    o **blocks:** Specifies input and output types (e.g., sequences and regression targets).
    o **get_x:** Extracts input features from the dataset.
    o **get_y:** Extracts target values from the dataset.
    o **splitter:** Splits the data into training and validation sets.
- **Output:** A DataBlock ready to create DataLoaders.

Example:

```
dblock = DataBlock(
    blocks=(InputBlock, RegressionBlock),
    get_x=lambda x: x[['lag_1', 'rolling_mean']],
    get_y=lambda x: x['value'],
    splitter=RandomSplitter(valid_pct=0.2)
)
```

Example Explanation:

- Defines `lag_1` and `rolling_mean` as input features and `value` as the target variable.
- Splits the dataset into training and validation subsets for model training.

4. Train the Model

What is Training the Model for Forecasting?

Training a forecasting model involves fitting a neural network to predict future values based on input features.

Syntax:

```
learn = tabular_learner(dls, layers=[100, 50],
metrics=rmse)
```

```
learn.fit_one_cycle(10, lr=1e-3)
```
Detailed Explanation:
- **Purpose:** Fits a neural network to the training data and evaluates it on validation data.
- **Parameters:**
  - `layers`: Specifies the architecture of the neural network.
  - `metrics`: Evaluation metrics like RMSE for regression tasks.
  - `lr`: Learning rate for optimization.
- **Output:** A trained model and validation metrics.

Example:
```
learn = tabular_learner(dls, layers=[200, 100],
metrics=rmse)
learn.fit_one_cycle(5, lr=3e-3)
```
Example Explanation:
- Trains a model with two hidden layers and monitors RMSE during training.
- Outputs training and validation metrics for each epoch.

5. Evaluate the Model

What is Evaluating the Model for Forecasting?

Evaluating a forecasting model involves comparing predicted values against true values to assess accuracy and reliability.

Syntax:
```
learn.show_results()
```
Detailed Explanation:
- **Purpose:** Displays a comparison of predicted and actual values for validation samples.
- **Parameters:**
  - None required for default behavior.
- **Output:** A table showing input features, true values, and predictions.**Example:**
```
learn.show_results()
```
Example Explanation:
- Highlights areas where the model performs well or needs improvement.
- Provides insights into prediction accuracy and potential areas for

refinement.

Real-Life Project:

Project Name: Forecasting Retail Sales

Project Goal: Build a model to forecast daily sales for a retail store based on historical data.

Code for This Project:

```python
from fastai.tabular.all import *
import pandas as pd
# Load dataset
data = pd.read_csv('retail_sales.csv',
parse_dates=['date'])
data['lag_1'] = data['sales'].shift(1)
data['rolling_mean'] =
data['sales'].rolling(window=7).mean()
data = data.dropna()
# Split dataset
splits = RandomSplitter(valid_pct=0.2)(range_of(data))
# Define DataBlock
dblock = DataBlock(
    blocks=(InputBlock, RegressionBlock),
    get_x=lambda x: x[['lag_1', 'rolling_mean']],
    get_y=lambda x: x['sales'],
    splitter=RandomSplitter(valid_pct=0.2)
)
# Create DataLoaders
dls = dblock.dataloaders(data)
# Initialize Learner
learn = tabular_learner(dls, layers=[200, 100],
metrics=rmse)
# Train the Model
learn.fit_one_cycle(10, lr=1e-2)

# Evaluate Results
learn.show_results()
```

Expected Output:

- Training and validation RMSE over multiple epochs.
- Predictions and actual values displayed for validation samples.

Chapter - 25 Handling Sequential Data in Fastai

Sequential data, characterized by its order and dependencies over time, plays a significant role in various domains such as finance, healthcare, and natural language processing. Fastai provides robust tools for handling sequential data, offering streamlined pipelines for preprocessing, modeling, and evaluation. This chapter explores the techniques and workflows to process and train models for sequential data using Fastai.

Key Characteristics of Handling Sequential Data in Fastai:

- **Temporal Dependencies:** Accommodates sequences where order matters.
- **Feature Engineering:** Extracts lags, rolling statistics, and time-based features.
- **Sequence Modeling:** Supports RNNs, LSTMs, and Transformer-based architectures.
- **Evaluation Metrics:** Tracks performance using task-appropriate metrics like MAE, MSE, and accuracy.

Basic Steps for Handling Sequential Data:

1. **Prepare the Dataset:** Load and preprocess sequential data.
2. **Engineer Features:** Create meaningful features that capture dependencies.
3. **Define DataBlock:** Specify input-output relationships for sequential tasks.
4. **Train Models:** Use sequential architectures like RNNs or Transformers.
5. **Evaluate Performance:** Assess and interpret model outputs.

Syntax Table:

SL No	Function	Syntax/Example	Description
1	Load Sequential Data	`pd.read_csv(filepath, parse_dates=...)`	Loads sequential data from a CSV file.
2	Feature Engineering	`df['lag'] = df['value'].shift(1)`	Creates lag features from the sequence.

3	Define DataBlock	`DataBlock(blocks, get_x, get_y, splitter)`	Prepares data for training and validation.
4	Train the Model	`learn.fit_one_cycle (...)`	Trains a sequential model.
5	Evaluate the Model	`learn.show_results( )`	Displays predictions alongside true values.

Syntax Explanation:

1. Load Sequential Data
What is Loading Sequential Data?
Loading sequential data involves importing temporal or ordered data from external sources and ensuring the sequence integrity is maintained.

Syntax:
```
import pandas as pd
data = pd.read_csv('sequential_data.csv',
parse_dates=['date'])
data.head()
```

Detailed Explanation:

- **Purpose:** Reads sequential data from a file into a Pandas DataFrame.
- **Parameters:**
  - `filepath`: Path to the CSV file containing sequential data.
  - `parse_dates`: Ensures specified columns are parsed as datetime objects.
- **Output:** A DataFrame with parsed datetime columns and the first few rows displayed for inspection.

Example:
```
data = pd.read_csv('stock_prices.csv',
parse_dates=['date'])
data.head()
```

Example Explanation:

- Loads stock price data with a `date` column parsed as datetime.
- Prepares the dataset for time-based operations, such as indexing and resampling.

2. Feature Engineering

What is Feature Engineering for Sequential Data?

Feature engineering enhances sequential data by creating derived features that capture temporal dependencies and patterns.

Syntax:

```
data['lag_1'] = data['value'].shift(1)
data['rolling_mean'] =
data['value'].rolling(window=3).mean()
```

Detailed Explanation:

- **Purpose:** Creates features such as lagged values and rolling averages to better model temporal relationships.
- **Parameters:**
  - `shift(n)`: Generates lagged features by shifting the sequence by n steps.
  - `rolling(window)`: Computes rolling statistics over a specified window size.
- **Output:** A DataFrame with additional columns for lagged values and rolling statistics.

Example:

```
data['lag_1'] = data['value'].shift(1)
data['rolling_mean'] =
data['value'].rolling(window=3).mean()
```

Example Explanation:

- Adds a lag feature (`lag_1`) and a rolling mean feature (`rolling_mean`) with a window size of 3.
- Captures short-term trends and dependencies in the sequence.

3. Define DataBlock

What is a Sequential DataBlock?

A Sequential DataBlock prepares temporal or ordered data for training and validation, defining how sequences and targets are extracted.

Syntax:

```
dblock = DataBlock(
    blocks=(InputBlock, RegressionBlock),
    get_x=lambda x: x[['features']],
    get_y=lambda x: x['target'],
    splitter=RandomSplitter(valid_pct=0.2)
```

)

Detailed Explanation:
- **Purpose:** Configures data processing for sequential modeling.
- **Parameters:**
  - blocks: Specifies input and output types (e.g., sequences and regression targets).
  - get_x: Extracts input features from the dataset.
  - get_y: Extracts target values from the dataset.
  - splitter: Splits the data into training and validation sets.
- **Output:** A DataBlock ready to create DataLoaders.

Example:
```
dblock = DataBlock(
    blocks=(InputBlock, RegressionBlock),
    get_x=lambda x: x[['lag_1', 'rolling_mean']],
    get_y=lambda x: x['value'],
    splitter=RandomSplitter(valid_pct=0.2)
)
```

Example Explanation:
- Defines lag_1 and rolling_mean as input features and value as the target variable.
- Splits the dataset into training and validation subsets for sequential modeling.

4. Train the Model

What is Training a Sequential Model?

Training a sequential model involves fitting a neural network to predict future values based on temporal input features.

Syntax:
```
learn = tabular_learner(dls, layers=[100, 50],
metrics=rmse)
learn.fit_one_cycle(10, lr=1e-3)
```
Detailed Explanation:

- **Purpose:** Trains a model on temporal data and evaluates its performance.

- **Parameters:**
  - o `layers`: Specifies the architecture of the neural network.
  - o `metrics`: Metrics like RMSE for regression tasks.
  - o `lr`: Learning rate for optimization.
- **Output:** A trained model with tracked metrics.

Example:
```
learn = tabular_learner(dls, layers=[200, 100],
metrics=rmse)
learn.fit_one_cycle(5, lr=3e-3)
```
Example Explanation:
- Trains a model with two hidden layers and monitors RMSE during training.
- Outputs training and validation metrics for each epoch.

5. Evaluate the Model
What is Evaluating a Sequential Model?
Evaluation compares predicted values against true values to measure the model's accuracy and reliability.

Syntax:
```
learn.show_results()
```
Detailed Explanation:

- **Purpose:** Displays a comparison of predicted and actual values for validation samples.
- **Parameters:**
  - o None required for default behavior.
- **Output:** A table showing input features, true values, and predictions.

Example:
```
learn.show_results()
```
Example Explanation:
- Highlights areas where the model performs well or needs improvement.
- Provides insights into prediction accuracy and potential areas for refinement.

Real-Life Project:

Project Name: Stock Price Prediction

Project Goal: Build a model to forecast daily stock prices based on historical data.

Code for This Project:

```python
from fastai.tabular.all import *
import pandas as pd
# Load dataset
data = pd.read_csv('stock_prices.csv',
parse_dates=['date'])
data['lag_1'] = data['close'].shift(1)
data['rolling_mean'] =
data['close'].rolling(window=7).mean()
data = data.dropna()
# Split dataset
splits = RandomSplitter(valid_pct=0.2)(range_of(data))
# Define DataBlock
dblock = DataBlock(
    blocks=(InputBlock, RegressionBlock),
    get_x=lambda x: x[['lag_1', 'rolling_mean']],
    get_y=lambda x: x['close'],
    splitter=RandomSplitter(valid_pct=0.2)
)
# Create DataLoaders
dls = dblock.dataloaders(data)
# Initialize Learner
learn = tabular_learner(dls, layers=[200, 100],
metrics=rmse)
# Train the Model
learn.fit_one_cycle(10, lr=1e-2)
# Evaluate Results
learn.show_results()
```

Expected Output:

- Training and validation RMSE over multiple epochs.
- Predictions and actual values displayed for validation samples.
- A trained model ready for deployment in sequential prediction tasks.

Chapter - 26 Predicting Customer Churn with Fastai

Customer churn prediction is a vital application in industries like telecommunications, banking, and e-commerce. It helps businesses identify customers likely to leave and take proactive retention measures. Fastai simplifies the process of building, training, and evaluating churn prediction models by providing tools for preprocessing, modeling, and interpretation. This chapter focuses on implementing customer churn prediction using Fastai.

Key Characteristics of Churn Prediction Models in Fastai:

- **Categorical and Continuous Feature Handling:** Seamlessly preprocesses and integrates diverse data types.
- **Built-In Pipelines:** Simplifies data handling with TabularDataBlock.
- **Customizable Neural Networks:** Supports flexible architectures tailored to churn prediction.
- **Integrated Metrics:** Tracks performance using accuracy, F1 score, or AUC.

Basic Steps for Customer Churn Prediction:

1. **Load and Inspect Data:** Import and explore customer data.
2. **Preprocess Features:** Handle missing values, encode categorical variables, and normalize continuous features.
3. **Define DataBlock:** Specify inputs, outputs, and transformations.
4. **Train the Model:** Build a neural network and train it for classification.
5. **Evaluate Performance:** Assess the model's performance and interpret its predictions.

Syntax Table:

SL No	Function	Syntax/Example	Description
1	Load Dataset	`pd.read_csv(filepath)`	Reads structured data from a CSV file.
2	Preprocess Data	`procs=[Categorify, FillMissing, Normalize()]`	Prepares data by encoding, filling, and scaling.
3	Define	`TabularDataBlock(..`	Configures the pipeline for

	DataBlock	`.)`	training and validation.
4	Train the Model	`learn.fit_one_cycle (...)`	Optimizes the model to predict churn.
5	Evaluate Results	`learn.show_results( )`	Displays predictions and actual values.

Syntax Explanation:

1. Load and Inspect Data
What is Loading and Inspecting Data?
Loading and inspecting data involves importing customer data into a Pandas DataFrame and exploring its structure and content.

Syntax:
```
import pandas as pd
data = pd.read_csv('customer_churn.csv')
data.head()
```

Detailed Explanation:
- **Purpose:** Reads structured customer data for further preprocessing.
- **Parameters:**
  - `filepath`: Path to the CSV file containing customer information.
- **Output:** A Pandas DataFrame displaying the first few rows for inspection.

Example:
```
data = pd.read_csv('churn_data.csv')
data.head()
```

Example Explanation:
- Loads customer churn data from `churn_data.csv`.
- Displays the first five rows to identify columns, data types, and missing values.

2. Preprocess Features
What is Preprocessing Features?

Preprocessing involves preparing data for model training by handling categorical and continuous variables and addressing missing values.

Syntax:

```
procs = [Categorify, FillMissing, Normalize]
```

Detailed Explanation:

- **Purpose:** Ensures data is in a format suitable for neural network training.
- **Components:**
    - `Categorify`: Encodes categorical variables into numerical indices.
    - `FillMissing`: Handles missing values in continuous columns.
    - `Normalize`: Scales continuous variables to have a mean of 0 and a standard deviation of 1.
- **Output:** Preprocessed data ready for training.

Example:

```
procs = [Categorify, FillMissing, Normalize]
```

Example Explanation:

- Configures preprocessing steps to encode categories, fill gaps, and normalize continuous variables.

3. Define DataBlock

What is a Tabular DataBlock?

A TabularDataBlock prepares customer data for training and validation, integrating preprocessing and feature selection.

Syntax:

```
dblock = TabularDataBlock(
    cat_names=['gender', 'region'],
    cont_names=['income', 'age'],
    y_names='churn',
    y_block=CategoryBlock(),
    procs=[Categorify, FillMissing, Normalize()],
    splits=splits
)
```

Detailed Explanation:

- **Purpose:** Configures data handling, including feature selection,

preprocessing, and dataset splitting.
- **Parameters:**
  - ○ `cat_names`: Lists categorical columns to encode.
  - ○ `cont_names`: Lists continuous columns to normalize.
  - ○ `y_names`: Specifies the target column for classification.
  - ○ `y_block`: Indicates the target type (e.g., `CategoryBlock` for classification).
  - ○ `procs`: Lists preprocessing functions to apply.
  - ○ `splits`: Divides the dataset into training and validation sets.
- **Output:** A DataBlock object ready to create DataLoaders.

Example:

```
dblock = TabularDataBlock(
    cat_names=['gender', 'region'],
    cont_names=['income', 'age'],
    y_names='churn',
    y_block=CategoryBlock(),
    procs=[Categorify, FillMissing, Normalize()],
    splits=splits
)
```

Example Explanation:
- Prepares a pipeline for customer data with `gender` and `region` as categorical features, `income` and `age` as continuous features, and `churn` as the target variable.
- Applies preprocessing steps and splits data for training and validation.

4. Train the Model

What is Training the Model?

Training involves fitting a neural network to classify customers as likely to churn or not based on input features.

Syntax:

```
learn = tabular_learner(dls, layers=[200, 100],
metrics=[accuracy, F1Score()])
learn.fit_one_cycle(10, lr=1e-2)
```

Detailed Explanation:

- **Purpose:** Optimizes model weights to minimize classification error.
- **Parameters:**
    - dls: DataLoaders containing preprocessed data.
    - layers: Specifies the architecture of the neural network.
    - metrics: Tracks performance metrics like accuracy and F1 score.
    - lr: Learning rate for gradient descent.
- **Output:** A trained model ready for evaluation.

Example:

```
learn = tabular_learner(dls, layers=[200, 100],
metrics=[accuracy, F1Score()])
learn.fit_one_cycle(10, lr=1e-2)
```

Example Explanation:
- Trains a neural network with two hidden layers and evaluates it using accuracy and F1 score.

5. Evaluate Performance

What is Evaluating Performance?

Evaluation compares the model's predictions against actual outcomes to assess its reliability.

Syntax:

```
learn.show_results()
```

Detailed Explanation:
- **Purpose:** Displays a comparison of predicted and true values for validation data.
- **Parameters:**
    - None required for default behavior.
- **Output:** A table showing input features, true labels, and predictions.

Example:

```
learn.show_results()
```

Example Explanation:
- Highlights where the model performs well and identifies potential areas for improvement.

Real-Life Project:

Project Name: Customer Churn Prediction for Subscription Services

Project Goal: Build a classification model to predict customer churn based on demographics, usage, and engagement.

Code for This Project:

```python
from fastai.tabular.all import *
import pandas as pd
# Load dataset
data = pd.read_csv('subscription_churn.csv')
# Split dataset
splits = RandomSplitter(valid_pct=0.2)(range_of(data))
# Define features
cat_names = ['gender', 'region', 'subscription_type']
cont_names = ['age', 'monthly_usage']
# Define DataBlock
dblock = TabularDataBlock(
    cat_names=cat_names,
    cont_names=cont_names,
    y_names='churn',
    y_block=CategoryBlock(),
    procs=[Categorify, FillMissing, Normalize()],
    splits=splits
)
# Create DataLoaders
dls = dblock.dataloaders(data)
# Initialize Learner
learn = tabular_learner(dls, layers=[200, 100],
metrics=[accuracy, F1Score()])
# Train the Model
learn.fit_one_cycle(10, lr=1e-2)
# Evaluate Results
learn.show_results()
```

Expected Output:

- Improved accuracy and F1 score over multiple epochs.
- Insights into key features driving churn predictions.
- A ready-to-deploy model for churn prediction.

Chapter - 27 Developing an Image Segmentation System with Fastai

Image segmentation is a crucial task in computer vision, where the goal is to classify each pixel of an image into specific categories. Applications range from medical imaging to autonomous driving. Fastai provides robust tools to streamline the creation of image segmentation models. This chapter explores how to develop and evaluate an image segmentation system using Fastai.

Key Characteristics of Image Segmentation in Fastai:

- **Pixel-Wise Classification:** Labels each pixel in an image for detailed analysis.
- **Predefined Architectures:** Supports state-of-the-art models like U-Net.
- **Flexible Data Pipelines:** Simplifies loading, augmenting, and preprocessing datasets.
- **Integrated Metrics:** Tracks performance using metrics like Dice score and IoU.

Basic Steps for Image Segmentation:

1. **Prepare the Dataset:** Load images and corresponding masks.
2. **Define DataBlock:** Specify input-output relationships and transformations.
3. **Train the Model:** Use a U-Net-based architecture for segmentation.
4. **Evaluate Performance:** Analyze segmentation quality using appropriate metrics.
5. **Interpret Results:** Visualize predictions and identify improvement areas.

Syntax Table:

SL No	Function	Syntax/Example	Description
1	Load Dataset	`get_image_files(path)`	Retrieves image files from a directory.
2	Define DataBlock	`DataBlock(blocks, get_items, splitter, ...)`	Configures dataset loading and transformations.

3	Create DataLoaders	`dblock.dataloaders(path)`	Converts the DataBlock into DataLoaders.
4	Train the Model	`unet_learner(dls, resnet34, metrics=...)`	Initializes a U-Net-based learner.
5	Evaluate Predictions	`learn.show_results(...)`	Displays predictions alongside true masks.

Syntax Explanation:

1. Load Dataset

What is Loading a Dataset?

Loading a dataset involves importing image files and their corresponding masks for segmentation tasks.

Syntax:

```
from fastai.vision.all import *
path = Path('path_to_dataset')
image_files = get_image_files(path/'images')
mask_files = get_image_files(path/'masks')
```

Detailed Explanation:

- **Purpose:** Retrieves image and mask files from specified directories.
- **Parameters:**
    - path: Path to the dataset directory.
    - `get_image_files`: Recursively collects image files from a directory.
- **Output:** Lists of image and mask file paths.

Example:

```
path = Path('segmentation_data')
image_files = get_image_files(path/'images')
mask_files = get_image_files(path/'masks')
```

Example Explanation:

- Gathers image files from images and corresponding mask files from masks.
- Prepares the dataset for DataBlock creation.

2. Define DataBlock

What is a DataBlock for Image Segmentation?

A DataBlock defines how images and masks are paired and processed for segmentation tasks.

Syntax:

```
def label_func(img_path):
    return path/'masks'/f"{img_path.stem}_mask.png"
dblock = DataBlock(
    blocks=(ImageBlock, MaskBlock(codes)),
    get_items=get_image_files,
    get_y=label_func,
    splitter=RandomSplitter(valid_pct=0.2),
    item_tfms=Resize(256),
    batch_tfms=aug_transforms()
)
```

Detailed Explanation:

- **Purpose:** Specifies input-output relationships and preprocessing steps for segmentation.
- **Parameters:**
    - `blocks`: Defines input (`ImageBlock`) and output (`MaskBlock`) types.
    - `get_items`: Function to retrieve image file paths.
    - `get_y`: Function to retrieve corresponding mask paths.
    - `splitter`: Splits data into training and validation sets.
    - `item_tfms`: Applies transformations like resizing at the item level.
    - `batch_tfms`: Applies augmentations like flipping and rotation at the batch level.
- **Output:** A DataBlock ready for DataLoader creation.

Example:

```
def label_func(img_path):
    return path/'masks'/f"{img_path.stem}_mask.png"
dblock = DataBlock(
    blocks=(ImageBlock, MaskBlock(codes)),
    get_items=get_image_files,
    get_y=label_func,
    splitter=RandomSplitter(valid_pct=0.2),
```

```
    item_tfms=Resize(256),
    batch_tfms=aug_transforms()
)
```
Example Explanation:

- Defines a DataBlock that pairs images with their masks using the `label_func` function.
- Resizes images and masks to 256x256 pixels and applies augmentations like flipping and brightness adjustments.

3. Create DataLoaders

What are DataLoaders?

DataLoaders manage batching and preprocessing, feeding data into the model during training and validation.

Syntax:
```
dls = dblock.dataloaders(path/'images')
```
Detailed Explanation:

- **Purpose:** Converts a DataBlock into DataLoaders for efficient training.
- **Parameters:**
    - path: Directory containing the image files.
- **Output:** DataLoaders ready for model training.

Example:
```
dls = dblock.dataloaders(path/'images')
```
Example Explanation:

- Creates DataLoaders for images and masks defined in the DataBlock.
- Facilitates data loading and preprocessing during training.

4. Train the Model

What is Training the Model?

Training involves fitting a neural network, such as a U-Net, to predict segmentation masks.

Syntax:
```
learn = unet_learner(dls, resnet34, metrics=Dice())
learn.fit_one_cycle(10, lr=1e-3)
```
Detailed Explanation:

- **Purpose:** Initializes and trains a U-Net-based segmentation model.

- **Parameters:**
  - o dls: DataLoaders containing images and masks.
  - o resnet34: Encoder architecture for the U-Net.
  - o metrics: Metric for evaluating segmentation quality (e.g., Dice score).
  - o lr: Learning rate for optimization.
- **Output:** A trained model and tracked metrics over training epochs.

Example:
```
learn = unet_learner(dls, resnet34, metrics=Dice())
learn.fit_one_cycle(10, lr=1e-3)
```
Example Explanation:

- Trains a U-Net model with a ResNet-34 backbone.
- Monitors Dice score during training to evaluate performance.

5. Evaluate Predictions

What is Evaluating Predictions?

Evaluation involves comparing predicted masks with true masks to assess segmentation quality.

Syntax:
```
learn.show_results(max_n=5)
```
Detailed Explanation:

- **Purpose:** Visualizes a batch of predicted and true masks.
- **Parameters:**
  - o max_n: Number of samples to display.
- **Output:** A grid of images, true masks, and predicted masks.

Example:
```
learn.show_results(max_n=3)
```
Example Explanation:

- Displays three samples with their corresponding true and predicted masks.
- Helps identify areas where the model performs well or struggles.

Real-Life Project:

Project Name: Medical Image Segmentation for Tumor Detection

Project Goal: Develop a system to segment tumors in medical images, aiding diagnosis.

Code for This Project:

```python
from fastai.vision.all import *

# Define dataset paths
path = Path('medical_images')

# Define label function
def label_func(img_path):
    return path/'masks'/f"{img_path.stem}_mask.png"
# Define DataBlock
dblock = DataBlock(
    blocks=(ImageBlock, MaskBlock(codes=['background',
'tumor'])),
    get_items=get_image_files,
    get_y=label_func,
    splitter=RandomSplitter(valid_pct=0.2),
    item_tfms=Resize(256),
    batch_tfms=aug_transforms()
)
# Create DataLoaders
dls = dblock.dataloaders(path/'images')

# Initialize Learner
learn = unet_learner(dls, resnet34, metrics=Dice())

# Train the Model
learn.fit_one_cycle(10, lr=1e-3)

# Evaluate Results
learn.show_results(max_n=5)
```

Expected Output:

- Improved Dice score over multiple epochs.
- Visualizations of predicted and true segmentation masks.
- A trained model ready for deployment in medical imaging tasks.

Chapter - 28 Creating a Sentiment Analysis Pipeline with Fastai

Sentiment analysis is a key application in natural language processing (NLP), enabling the extraction of opinions, emotions, or sentiments from text. Fastai simplifies building sentiment analysis pipelines with pre-trained language models, data preprocessing tools, and intuitive APIs. This chapter explores the steps for creating and deploying a sentiment analysis pipeline using Fastai.

Key Characteristics of a Sentiment Analysis Pipeline in Fastai:

- **Pretrained Models:** Leverages state-of-the-art language models like AWD-LSTM or Transformer architectures.
- **Data Preprocessing:** Tokenizes and numericalizes text data efficiently.
- **Fine-Tuning:** Allows transfer learning for domain-specific sentiment tasks.
- **Evaluation Metrics:** Tracks accuracy, F1 score, or other metrics to measure performance.

Basic Steps for Sentiment Analysis:

1. **Prepare the Dataset:** Load and preprocess text data.
2. **Tokenize and Numericalize:** Convert text into tokens and numerical representations.
3. **Define DataBlock:** Specify input-output relationships for sentiment classification.
4. **Fine-Tune the Model:** Use transfer learning for sentiment classification.
5. **Evaluate Performance:** Test the model and interpret results.

Syntax Table:

SL No	Function	Syntax/Example	Description
1	Load Dataset	`pd.read_csv(filepath)`	Reads text data from a CSV file.
2	Tokenize Text	`TextBlock.from_df(...)`	Tokenizes text data from a DataFrame column.
3	Define	`DataBlock(...`	Prepares data for training

		DataBlock	)	and validation.
4	Fine-Tune the Model	`text_classifi er_learner(.. .)`	Initializes a learner for text classification.
5	Evaluate Results	`learn.show_re sults()`	Displays predictions alongside actual labels.

Syntax Explanation:

1. Load and Inspect Dataset
What is Loading and Inspecting a Dataset?
Loading and inspecting data involves importing text data into a Pandas DataFrame and exploring its structure.
Syntax:
```
import pandas as pd
data = pd.read_csv('sentiment_data.csv')
data.head()
```
Detailed Explanation:
- **Purpose:** Reads text data and labels from a CSV file for preprocessing.
- **Parameters:**
    - `filepath`: Path to the CSV file containing text and sentiment labels.
- **Output:** A Pandas DataFrame with the first few rows displayed for inspection.

Example:
```
data = pd.read_csv('reviews.csv')
data.head()
```
Example Explanation:
- Loads review data from `reviews.csv`.
- Displays the first five rows to verify columns and data structure.

2. Tokenize and Numericalize
What is Tokenization and Numericalization?
Tokenization splits text into smaller units (tokens), and numericalization converts these tokens into numbers for model input.
Syntax:

```
TextBlock.from_df('text_column', is_lm=False)
```
Detailed Explanation:

- **Purpose:** Prepares text data for input to a language model or classifier.
- **Parameters:**
    - `text_column`: Name of the DataFrame column containing text.
    - `is_lm`: Set to `False` for classification tasks.
- **Output:** A `TextBlock` that processes text data during DataLoader creation.

Example:
```
text_block = TextBlock.from_df('review', is_lm=False)
```
Example Explanation:

- Processes the `review` column for text classification.
- Converts raw text into tokenized and numericalized format.

3. Define DataBlock

What is a Sentiment Analysis DataBlock?

A DataBlock configures how text and labels are paired, processed, and split for training and validation.

Syntax:
```
dblock = DataBlock(
    blocks=(TextBlock.from_df('text_column'),
CategoryBlock),
    get_x=ColReader('text_column'),
    get_y=ColReader('label_column'),
    splitter=RandomSplitter(valid_pct=0.2)
)
```

Detailed Explanation:

- **Purpose:** Prepares text and labels for training.
- **Parameters:**
    - `blocks`: Specifies input (`TextBlock`) and output (`CategoryBlock`) types.
    - `get_x`: Extracts text from the specified column.
    - `get_y`: Extracts labels from the specified column.
    - `splitter`: Splits data into training and validation sets.

- **Output:** A DataBlock ready for DataLoader creation.

Example:
```
dblock = DataBlock(
    blocks=(TextBlock.from_df('review'),
CategoryBlock),
    get_x=ColReader('review'),
    get_y=ColReader('sentiment'),
    splitter=RandomSplitter(valid_pct=0.2)
)
```

Example Explanation:
- Configures a DataBlock for sentiment analysis using review as text input and sentiment as labels.
- Splits 20% of data into a validation set.

4. Fine-Tune the Model

What is Fine-Tuning the Model?

Fine-tuning involves adapting a pre-trained language model to a specific task like sentiment analysis.

Syntax:
```
learn = text_classifier_learner(dls, AWD_LSTM,
metrics=accuracy)
learn.fine_tune(4, base_lr=1e-3)
```

Detailed Explanation:
- **Purpose:** Initializes and fine-tunes a text classification model.
- **Parameters:**
    - dls: DataLoaders containing preprocessed data.
    - AWD_LSTM: Pretrained language model architecture.
    - metrics: Metrics like accuracy to evaluate performance.
    - base_lr: Learning rate for fine-tuning.
- **Output:** A trained sentiment analysis model.

Example:
```
learn = text_classifier_learner(dls, AWD_LSTM,
metrics=accuracy)
learn.fine_tune(4, base_lr=1e-3)
```

Example Explanation:
- Fine-tunes an AWD-LSTM model for four epochs with a learning rate of 0.001.

- Tracks accuracy during training.

5. Evaluate Performance

What is Evaluating Performance?

Evaluation compares model predictions against true labels to assess accuracy and reliability.

Syntax:

```
learn.show_results()
```

Detailed Explanation:

- **Purpose:** Displays predictions alongside actual labels for validation samples.
- **Parameters:**
  - None required for default behavior.
- **Output:** A table of input text, true labels, and predicted labels.

Example:

```
learn.show_results(max_n=5)
```

Example Explanation:

- Displays five validation samples with their predictions.
- Helps identify patterns in errors or misclassifications.

Real-Life Project:

Project Name: Sentiment Analysis for Product Reviews

Project Goal: Build a sentiment analysis pipeline to classify product reviews as positive, negative, or neutral.

Code for This Project:

```python
from fastai.text.all import *
import pandas as pd
# Load dataset
data = pd.read_csv('product_reviews.csv')
# Define DataBlock
dblock = DataBlock(
    blocks=(TextBlock.from_df('review'),
CategoryBlock),
    get_x=ColReader('review'),
    get_y=ColReader('sentiment'),
    splitter=RandomSplitter(valid_pct=0.2)
)
# Create DataLoaders
```

```
dls = dblock.dataloaders(data)

# Initialize Learner
learn = text_classifier_learner(dls, AWD_LSTM,
metrics=[accuracy, F1Score()])

# Fine-Tune the Model
learn.fine_tune(4, base_lr=1e-3)

# Evaluate Results
learn.show_results(max_n=5)
```

Expected Output:
- Improved accuracy and F1 score over multiple epochs.
- Predictions for validation samples displayed alongside true labels.
- A trained model ready for deployment in sentiment analysis tasks.

Chapter - 29 Building a Recommendation System with Fastai

Recommendation systems are essential in modern applications such as e-commerce, streaming platforms, and social networks. They predict user preferences and suggest relevant items, improving user engagement and satisfaction. Fastai provides a robust framework for developing recommendation systems, leveraging collaborative filtering and neural network techniques. This chapter guides you through building a recommendation system using Fastai.

Key Characteristics of Recommendation Systems in Fastai:

- **Collaborative Filtering:** Uses user-item interactions to predict preferences.
- **Pretrained Embeddings:** Learns latent factors for users and items.
- **Customizability:** Supports extending models with additional features.
- **Integrated Metrics:** Evaluates performance with metrics like RMSE.

Basic Steps for Building a Recommendation System:

1. **Prepare the Dataset:** Load and preprocess user-item interaction data.
2. **Define DataBlock:** Specify how to organize and process the data.
3. **Train the Model:** Use Fastai's `collab_learner` for collaborative filtering.
4. **Evaluate Performance:** Analyze the model's accuracy and errors.
5. **Make Predictions:** Generate recommendations for users.

Syntax Table:

SL No	Function	Syntax/Example	Description
1	Load Dataset	`pd.read_csv(filepath)`	Reads interaction data from a CSV file.
2	Define DataBlock	`DataBlock(blocks, get_x, get_y, splitter)`	Prepares data for training and validation.
3	Train the Model	`collab_learner(...)`	Initializes a collaborative filtering learner.

| 4 | Evaluate Results | `learn.show_results(...)` | Displays predictions alongside actual values. |
| 5 | Generate Predictions | `learn.predict(...)` | Predicts preferences for a user-item pair. |

Syntax Explanation:

1. Prepare the Dataset

What is Preparing the Dataset?

Preparing the dataset involves importing user-item interaction data into a Pandas DataFrame and verifying its structure.

Syntax:

```
import pandas as pd
data = pd.read_csv('user_ratings.csv')
data.head()
```

Detailed Explanation:

- **Purpose:** Loads user-item interaction data for preprocessing.
- **Parameters:**
    - `filepath`: Path to the CSV file containing user-item ratings or interactions.
- **Output:** A DataFrame displaying the first few rows for inspection.

Example:

```
data = pd.read_csv('ratings.csv')
data.head()
```

Example Explanation:

- Reads `ratings.csv` containing columns like `user_id`, `item_id`, and `rating`.
- Displays the first five rows to verify data structure.

2. Define DataBlock

What is a DataBlock for Recommendations?

A DataBlock specifies how user-item interactions are processed and split into training and validation sets.

Syntax:

```
dblock = DataBlock(
    blocks=(CollabBlock),
    get_x=ColReader('user_id'),
```

```
    get_y=ColReader('rating'),
    splitter=RandomSplitter(valid_pct=0.2)
)
```

Detailed Explanation:

- **Purpose:** Configures how user-item pairs and ratings are handled.
- **Parameters:**
    - blocks: Specifies input and output types (e.g., CollabBlock for collaborative filtering).
    - get_x: Extracts user or item identifiers.
    - get_y: Extracts the target column (e.g., ratings).
    - splitter: Splits data into training and validation sets.
- **Output:** A DataBlock ready to create DataLoaders.

Example:

```
dblock = DataBlock(
    blocks=(CollabBlock),
    get_x=ColReader(['user_id', 'item_id']),
    get_y=ColReader('rating'),
    splitter=RandomSplitter(valid_pct=0.2)
)
```

Example Explanation:

- Configures a DataBlock for user-item pairs and ratings.
- Splits 20% of the data into a validation set.

3. Train the Model

What is Training the Model?
Training involves fitting a collaborative filtering model to predict user-item ratings.

Syntax:

```
learn = collab_learner(dls, y_range=(0.5, 5.0),
metrics=rmse)
learn.fit_one_cycle(5, lr=5e-3)
```

Detailed Explanation:

- **Purpose:** Learns embeddings for users and items to predict ratings.
- **Parameters:**
    - dls: DataLoaders containing training and validation data.

- o   y_range: Range of target values (e.g., rating scale from 0.5 to 5.0).
- o   metrics: Tracks performance metrics like RMSE.
- o   lr: Learning rate for optimization.
- **Output:** A trained collaborative filtering model.

Example:
```
learn = collab_learner(dls, y_range=(0.5, 5.0),
metrics=rmse)
learn.fit_one_cycle(5, lr=5e-3)
```
Example Explanation:
- Trains a collaborative filtering model for five epochs with an initial learning rate of 0.005.
- Monitors RMSE to assess prediction accuracy.

4. Evaluate Results

What is Evaluating Results?
Evaluation compares model predictions with actual ratings to assess accuracy and reliability.
Syntax:
```
learn.show_results(max_n=5)
```
Detailed Explanation:
- **Purpose:** Displays predicted and true ratings for validation samples.
- **Parameters:**
  - o   max_n: Number of samples to display.
- **Output:** A table showing user-item pairs, true ratings, and predicted ratings.

Example:
```
learn.show_results(max_n=5)
```
Example Explanation:
- Displays five validation samples with predicted and actual ratings.
- Identifies where the model performs well or needs improvement.

5. Generate Predictions

What is Generating Predictions?

Generating predictions involves estimating ratings for specific user-item pairs or recommending items to users.

Syntax:
```
learn.predict((user_id, item_id))
```

Detailed Explanation:
- **Purpose:** Predicts the rating for a given user-item pair.
- **Parameters:**
  - `(user_id, item_id)`: Pair for which the rating is predicted.
- **Output:** The predicted rating.

Example:
```
learn.predict((42, 101))
```

Example Explanation:
- Predicts the rating for user ID 42 and item ID 101.
- Provides insights into the model's recommendations.

Real-Life Project:

Project Name: Personalized Movie Recommendation System

Project Goal: Build a system to recommend movies to users based on their ratings and preferences.

Code for This Project:
```python
from fastai.collab import *
from fastai.tabular.all import *
import pandas as pd

# Load dataset
data = pd.read_csv('movie_ratings.csv')

# Define DataBlock
dblock = DataBlock(
    blocks=(CollabBlock),
    get_x=ColReader(['user_id', 'movie_id']),
    get_y=ColReader('rating'),
    splitter=RandomSplitter(valid_pct=0.2)
)
# Create DataLoaders
```

```
dls = dblock.dataloaders(data)

# Initialize Learner
learn = collab_learner(dls, y_range=(0.5, 5.0),
metrics=rmse)

# Train the Model
learn.fit_one_cycle(5, lr=5e-3)

# Evaluate Results
learn.show_results(max_n=5)

# Generate a Prediction
predicted_rating = learn.predict((user_id, movie_id))
print(predicted_rating)
```
Expected Output:
- RMSE improvement over multiple epochs.
- Predictions for user-item pairs displayed alongside actual ratings.
- A functional model capable of recommending movies to users.

Chapter - 29 Time Series Forecasting for Sales Data with Fastai

Time series forecasting is a critical task in various industries to predict future values based on historical data. Sales data forecasting is particularly useful for inventory management, financial planning, and demand prediction. Fastai offers powerful tools to build and fine-tune forecasting models using sequence-based architectures. This chapter walks through creating a time series forecasting model for sales data using Fastai.

Key Characteristics of Time Series Forecasting with Fastai:

- **Sequential Data Handling:** Accommodates dependencies in temporal data.
- **Feature Engineering:** Supports time-based feature extraction like lags and rolling statistics.
- **Prebuilt Architectures:** Leverages models such as LSTMs and Transformers for sequence prediction.
- **Performance Metrics:** Tracks accuracy using metrics like MSE, RMSE, and MAE.

Basic Steps for Time Series Forecasting:

1. **Load and Inspect Data:** Import and examine the sales dataset.
2. **Engineer Features:** Extract meaningful features from the time series.
3. **Define DataBlock:** Specify input-output relationships for forecasting.
4. **Train the Model:** Use sequential models to predict future sales.
5. **Evaluate Performance:** Analyze results and refine the model.

Syntax Table:

SL No	Function	Syntax/Example	Description
1	Load Dataset	`pd.read_csv(filepath, parse_dates=...)`	Reads sales data from a CSV file.
2	Feature Engineering	`df['lag'] = df['value'].shift(1)`	Creates lag features for temporal dependencies.
3	Define	`DataBlock(blocks,`	Prepares data for training

	DataBlock	get_x, get_y, splitter)	and validation.
4	Train the Model	learn.fit_one_cycl e(...)	Fits the model to the data.
5	Evaluate Results	learn.show_results ()	Displays predictions alongside actual values.

Syntax Explanation:

1. Load and Inspect Data

What is Loading and Inspecting Data?

This step involves importing time series data into a Pandas DataFrame and verifying its structure.

Syntax:

```
import pandas as pd
data = pd.read_csv('sales_data.csv',
parse_dates=['date'])
data.head()
```

Detailed Explanation:

- **Purpose:** Reads time series data for preprocessing and exploration.
- **Parameters:**
    - o filepath: Path to the sales data file.
    - o parse_dates: Parses date columns as datetime objects.
- **Output:** A DataFrame displaying the first few rows for inspection.

Example:

```
data = pd.read_csv('monthly_sales.csv',
parse_dates=['date'])
data.head()
```

Example Explanation:

- Loads monthly sales data with a date column for temporal analysis.
- Verifies the structure and content of the dataset.

2. Engineer Features

What is Feature Engineering?

Feature engineering creates additional columns that capture temporal patterns, such as lags, moving averages, and seasonal indicators.

Syntax:

```
data['lag_1'] = data['sales'].shift(1)
data['rolling_mean'] =
data['sales'].rolling(window=3).mean()
```
Detailed Explanation:

- **Purpose:** Enhances the dataset with features that model temporal relationships.
- **Parameters:**
  - `shift(n)`: Creates lagged features by shifting values by n time steps.
  - `rolling(window)`: Computes rolling statistics over a defined window.
- **Output:** A DataFrame with additional features.

Example:
```
data['lag_1'] = data['sales'].shift(1)
data['rolling_mean'] =
data['sales'].rolling(window=3).mean()
```
Example Explanation:

- Adds a lag feature (`lag_1`) and a 3-period rolling mean (`rolling_mean`).
- Captures short-term trends in sales data.

3. Define DataBlock

What is a DataBlock for Time Series Forecasting?

A DataBlock organizes temporal data for training and validation, defining how sequences and targets are extracted.

Syntax:
```
dblock = DataBlock(
    blocks=(InputBlock, RegressionBlock),
    get_x=lambda x: x[['lag_1', 'rolling_mean']],
    get_y=lambda x: x['sales'],
    splitter=RandomSplitter(valid_pct=0.2)
)
```
Detailed Explanation:

- **Purpose:** Configures data processing for time series modeling.
- **Parameters:**
  - `blocks`: Specifies input (features) and output (target)

types.
- o get_x: Extracts feature columns.
- o get_y: Extracts target column.
- o splitter: Splits data into training and validation sets.
- **Output:** A DataBlock ready for DataLoader creation.

Example:
```
dblock = DataBlock(
    blocks=(InputBlock, RegressionBlock),
    get_x=lambda x: x[['lag_1', 'rolling_mean']],
    get_y=lambda x: x['sales'],
    splitter=RandomSplitter(valid_pct=0.2)
)
```
Example Explanation:
- Prepares a pipeline for sales data using lag and rolling mean as input features and sales as the target.
- Splits 20% of the data for validation.

4. Train the Model

What is Training the Model?

Training a time series model involves fitting a neural network to predict future sales based on input features.

Syntax:
```
learn = tabular_learner(dls, layers=[100, 50],
metrics=rmse)
learn.fit_one_cycle(10, lr=1e-3)
```
Detailed Explanation:
- **Purpose:** Optimizes model weights to minimize prediction error.
- **Parameters:**
  - o dls: DataLoaders for training and validation.
  - o layers: Defines the architecture of the neural network.
  - o metrics: Evaluation metrics, such as RMSE.
  - o lr: Learning rate for optimization.
- **Output:** A trained model with tracked metrics.

Example:
```
learn = tabular_learner(dls, layers=[200, 100],
metrics=rmse)
learn.fit_one_cycle(5, lr=3e-3)
```

Example Explanation:

- Trains a model with two hidden layers and tracks RMSE to evaluate performance.

5. Evaluate Results

What is Evaluating Results?

Evaluation compares predicted and actual sales to assess the model's accuracy and reliability.

Syntax:

```
learn.show_results()
```

Detailed Explanation:

- **Purpose:** Displays predictions alongside true values for validation samples.
- **Parameters:**
  - None required for default behavior.
- **Output:** A table showing input features, actual values, and predictions.

Example:

```
learn.show_results()
```

Example Explanation:

- Highlights areas where the model performs well or needs improvement.
- Provides insights into forecast accuracy.

Real-Life Project:

Project Name: Monthly Sales Forecasting

Project Goal: Build a forecasting model to predict monthly sales for a retail store.

Code for This Project:

```
from fastai.tabular.all import *
import pandas as pd

# Load dataset
data = pd.read_csv('monthly_sales.csv',
parse_dates=['date'])
data['lag_1'] = data['sales'].shift(1)
data['rolling_mean'] =
data['sales'].rolling(window=3).mean()
```

```
data = data.dropna()

# Split dataset
splits = RandomSplitter(valid_pct=0.2)(range_of(data))

# Define DataBlock
dblock = DataBlock(
    blocks=(InputBlock, RegressionBlock),
    get_x=lambda x: x[['lag_1', 'rolling_mean']],
    get_y=lambda x: x['sales'],
    splitter=RandomSplitter(valid_pct=0.2)
)
# Create DataLoaders
dls = dblock.dataloaders(data)
# Initialize Learner
learn = tabular_learner(dls, layers=[200, 100],
metrics=rmse)
# Train the Model
learn.fit_one_cycle(10, lr=1e-2)
# Evaluate Results
learn.show_results()
```

Expected Output:
- Improved RMSE over multiple epochs.
- Predictions and actual sales displayed for validation samples.
- A trained model ready for deployment in forecasting tasks.

Chapter - 30 Exporting Models for Inference with Fastai

Once a machine learning model is trained, exporting it for inference is a critical step to enable deployment in real-world applications. Fastai simplifies the process of exporting models, ensuring that they can be efficiently loaded and used for predictions across various platforms. This chapter explains how to export models for inference using Fastai.

Key Characteristics of Model Exporting in Fastai:

- **Efficiency:** Preserves the trained model's architecture and parameters.
- **Compatibility:** Supports deployment in different environments.
- **Ease of Use:** Integrates seamlessly with Fastai's Learner class.
- **Cross-Platform:** Enables usage in Python applications and beyond.

Basic Steps for Exporting Models:

1. **Train the Model:** Fit the model on the training data.
2. **Export the Model:** Save the model in a platform-agnostic format.
3. **Load the Model:** Reload the model for inference.
4. **Make Predictions:** Use the loaded model to make predictions on new data.

Syntax Table:

SL No	Function	Syntax/Example	Description
1	Export Model	`learn.export(fname)`	Saves the trained model to a file.
2	Load Exported Model	`load_learner(fname)`	Loads a previously exported model.
3	Make Predictions	`learn.predict(data)`	Predicts the output for new input data.

Syntax Explanation:

1. Export the Model

What is Exporting the Model?

Exporting the model saves the trained model, including its architecture and parameters, to a file for later use.

Syntax:

```
learn.export(fname='model.pkl')
```

Detailed Explanation:

- **Purpose:** Preserves the trained model in a file that can be reloaded for inference.
- **Parameters:**
  - fname: File name or path to save the model (default is `export.pkl`).
- **Output:** A file containing the exported model.

Example:

```
learn.export(fname='sales_forecasting_model.pkl')
```

Example Explanation:

- Saves the trained model to a file named `sales_forecasting_model.pkl`.
- Prepares the model for deployment or further use.

2. Load the Exported Model

What is Loading an Exported Model?
Loading an exported model allows you to restore the model for inference without retraining.

Syntax:

```
learn = load_learner(fname='model.pkl')
```

Detailed Explanation:

- **Purpose:** Restores a previously exported model, including its architecture and parameters.
- **Parameters:**
  - fname: File name or path of the exported model.
- **Output:** A Learner object ready for inference.

Example:

```
learn =
load_learner(fname='sales_forecasting_model.pkl')
```

Example Explanation:

- Loads the `sales_forecasting_model.pkl` file into a Learner object.
- Makes the model ready for making predictions.

3. Make Predictions

What is Making Predictions?
Making predictions involves using the loaded model to generate outputs for new input data.

Syntax:
```
pred = learn.predict(data)
```

Detailed Explanation:

- **Purpose:** Uses the loaded model to infer outcomes based on new data.
- **Parameters:**
    - data: Input data for which predictions are required.
- **Output:** Predicted value(s) and additional details like probabilities (for classification).

Example:
```
new_data = pd.DataFrame({'lag_1': [200],
'rolling_mean': [210]})
pred = learn.predict(new_data.iloc[0])
print(pred)
```

Example Explanation:

- Predicts the future sales for given input features lag_1 and rolling_mean.
- Outputs the predicted value and confidence intervals (if applicable).

Real-Life Project:
Project Name: Deploying a Sales Forecasting Model
Project Goal: Export and deploy a trained sales forecasting model to make predictions for inventory management.
Code for This Project:
```
from fastai.tabular.all import *
import pandas as pd

# Load dataset
data = pd.read_csv('monthly_sales.csv',
parse_dates=['date'])
```

```python
data['lag_1'] = data['sales'].shift(1)
data['rolling_mean'] =
data['sales'].rolling(window=3).mean()
data = data.dropna()
# Split dataset
splits = RandomSplitter(valid_pct=0.2)(range_of(data))
# Define DataBlock
dblock = DataBlock(
    blocks=(InputBlock, RegressionBlock),
    get_x=lambda x: x[['lag_1', 'rolling_mean']],
    get_y=lambda x: x['sales'],
    splitter=RandomSplitter(valid_pct=0.2)
)
# Create DataLoaders
dls = dblock.dataloaders(data)
# Initialize Learner
learn = tabular_learner(dls, layers=[200, 100],
metrics=rmse)
# Train the Model
learn.fit_one_cycle(10, lr=1e-2)
# Export the Model
learn.export(fname='sales_forecasting_model.pkl')
# Load the Model for Inference
learn =
load_learner(fname='sales_forecasting_model.pkl')
# Make a Prediction
new_data = pd.DataFrame({'lag_1': [200],
'rolling_mean': [210]})
pred = learn.predict(new_data.iloc[0])
print(f"Predicted Sales: {pred}")
```
Expected Output:

- A model file sales_forecasting_model.pkl is created for deployment.
- Predictions for new input data are generated efficiently.
- A ready-to-use model for real-world forecasting tasks.

Chapter - 31 Deploying Fastai Models with Flask and FastAPI

After training and exporting a machine learning model, deploying it as a web service enables users to interact with the model in real-world applications. Flask and FastAPI are popular Python frameworks for building web APIs. This chapter provides step-by-step instructions on deploying Fastai models using Flask and FastAPI.

Key Characteristics of Deployment Frameworks:

- **Flask:** Simple and lightweight for building RESTful APIs.
- **FastAPI:** High-performance, asynchronous, and supports automatic documentation.
- **Integration:** Both frameworks seamlessly load and interact with Fastai models.
- **Scalability:** Suitable for small prototypes to production-grade systems.

Basic Steps for Deployment:

1. **Export the Model:** Save the trained model using `learn.export()`.
2. **Set Up the Framework:** Create a Flask or FastAPI application.
3. **Load the Model:** Use `load_learner()` to restore the exported model.
4. **Define API Endpoints:** Configure routes for inference.
5. **Run and Test the Service:** Host the application and validate predictions.

Using Flask for Deployment

1. Export the Model

Ensure the trained model is exported for inference:

```
learn.export(fname='model.pkl')
```

2. Create a Flask Application

Install Flask:

```
pip install flask
```

Define the Flask app:

```python
from flask import Flask, request, jsonify
from fastai.learner import load_learner

# Load the exported model
model = load_learner('model.pkl')

# Initialize Flask app
app = Flask(__name__)

@app.route('/predict', methods=['POST'])
def predict():
    data = request.json
    pred = model.predict(data['input'])
    return jsonify({'prediction': str(pred[0])})

if __name__ == '__main__':
    app.run(debug=True)
```

3. Run the Flask Application

Save the script (e.g., `app.py`) and run:

```
python app.py
```

Access the API at http://127.0.0.1:5000/predict.

4. Test the Flask API

Use a tool like `curl` or Postman to test the endpoint:

```
curl -X POST -H "Content-Type: application/json" -d
'{"input": [200, 210]}' http://127.0.0.1:5000/predict
```

Using FastAPI for Deployment

1. Export the Model

Export the trained model as before:

```
learn.export(fname='model.pkl')
```

2. Create a FastAPI Application

Install FastAPI and Uvicorn:

```
pip install fastapi uvicorn
```

Define the FastAPI app:

```python
from fastapi import FastAPI
from pydantic import BaseModel
from fastai.learner import load_learner
# Load the exported model
```

```python
model = load_learner('model.pkl')
# Initialize FastAPI app
app = FastAPI()
# Define input schema
class PredictionRequest(BaseModel):
    lag_1: float
    rolling_mean: float
@app.post('/predict')
def predict(request: PredictionRequest):
    data = [request.lag_1, request.rolling_mean]
    pred = model.predict(data)
    return {"prediction": str(pred[0])}
```

3. Run the FastAPI Application
Save the script (e.g., `main.py`) and run:
```
uvicorn main:app --reload
```

Access the API at http://127.0.0.1:8000/predict.

4. Test the FastAPI Endpoint
Use `curl` or Postman to test the API:
```
curl -X POST -H "Content-Type: application/json" -d
'{"lag_1": 200, "rolling_mean": 210}'
http://127.0.0.1:8000/predict
```

5. API Documentation
FastAPI automatically generates interactive documentation. Access it at:
- Swagger UI: http://127.0.0.1:8000/docs
- ReDoc: http://127.0.0.1:8000/redoc

Real-Life Project:

Project Name: Deploying a Forecasting API

Project Goal: Deploy a sales forecasting model as a web service accessible through RESTful APIs.

Code for Flask Deployment:
```python
from flask import Flask, request, jsonify
from fastai.learner import load_learner

# Load the exported model
model = load_learner('sales_forecasting_model.pkl')
```

```python
# Initialize Flask app
app = Flask(__name__)

@app.route('/predict', methods=['POST'])
def predict():
    data = request.json
    pred = model.predict([data['lag_1'],
data['rolling_mean']])
    return jsonify({'prediction': str(pred[0])})

if __name__ == '__main__':
    app.run(debug=True)
```

Code for FastAPI Deployment:

```python
from fastapi import FastAPI
from pydantic import BaseModel
from fastai.learner import load_learner

# Load the exported model
model = load_learner('sales_forecasting_model.pkl')
# Initialize FastAPI app
app = FastAPI()

# Define input schema
class PredictionRequest(BaseModel):
    lag_1: float
    rolling_mean: float

@app.post('/predict')
def predict(request: PredictionRequest):
    data = [request.lag_1, request.rolling_mean]
    pred = model.predict(data)
    return {"prediction": str(pred[0])}
```

Expected Output:

- APIs hosted locally or on a server.
- Interactive endpoints for making predictions.
- Documentation generated automatically for FastAPI applications.

www.ingramcontent.com/pod-product-compliance
Lightning Source LLC
LaVergne TN
LVHW051328050326
832903LV00031B/3419